MARRIAGE SUCCESS
SECRETS

*THE ULTIMATE GUIDE FOR A FULFILLING
MARRIAGE*

BY
EDOUARD ATANGANA

COPYRIGHTS

Acknowledgment

As I reflect on the journey of writing "Marriage Success Secrets: An Ultimate Guide for a Fulfilling Marriage," my heart is filled with immense gratitude for the myriad of individuals whose experiences, wisdom, and support have made this book a reality.

First and foremost, I owe a debt of gratitude to the many families who have generously shared their marital experiences with me in my pastoral work. Your openness and honesty have not only inspired this book but have also enriched my understanding of the beauty and complexities of marital life.

To my married friends, your willingness to teach me the many facets of marital life has been invaluable. Your lives are a testament to the joys and challenges of marriage, and your stories have been a guiding light in my writing.

My studies in social sciences have been instrumental in shaping my perspectives on the different stages of marriages and the consequential behaviors. I am grateful for the academic journey that has allowed me to explore these facets in depth, providing a solid foundation for the insights shared in this book.

A special note of thanks goes to the editorial and publishing team whose expertise transformed my manuscript into the book it is today. Your professionalism, insight, and patience have been remarkable, and I am deeply appreciative of your commitment to this project.

To all the couples whose marriages I have had the honor of preparing and officiating, you are the heartbeat of this book. Your journeys, celebrations, and enduring love have not only inspired me but also countless others who will find guidance and hope in these pages.

In closing, I extend my heartfelt thanks to everyone who has been a part of this journey. Your contributions, in myriad ways, have helped bring "Marriage Success Secrets" to life, and for that, I am eternally grateful.

With warm regards and blessings,

Edouard Atangana

McAllen, January 2024

DEDICATION

This book is lovingly dedicated to:

Patty and Tony Alanis

Lourdes and Manolo Galvan

Mirta and Gerardo Rocha

Viola and Robert Garcia

Your marriages stand as beacons of love, commitment, and endurance in a world where such virtues are increasingly precious. Through the years, you have not only nurtured the bond you share with your spouses but have also served as inspiring examples of what it means to love, honor, and cherish one another in both joyful and challenging times.

Your journeys, filled with shared laughter, tears, dreams, and the quiet strength of partnership, have illuminated the path for others to follow. This book, in many ways, is a reflection of the wisdom and grace found in your enduring unions.

May your love continue to flourish and may your lives always be filled with the joy and peace that come from a deep and abiding partnership.

With deepest respect and admiration,

Fr. Edouard Atangana, PhD, STL

Prologue

In the year 2014, a remarkable 88% of Americans professed to marry for love, reaffirming the enduring belief that love serves as the cornerstone of a prosperous marriage. An overwhelming 81% emphasized that marriage transcends mere short-term engagements, emphasizing its profound significance within American society. These statistics reflect an undeniable truth: despite societal shifts and evolving attitudes, marriage remains a cherished and significant institution in American culture. Approximately 85% of adults are expected to enter marriage at some point in their lives, illustrating its enduring allure and relevance.

However, amidst this commitment to love and lifelong partnership, a paradox emerges—the United States holds a high divorce rate. Recent research paints a stark picture, revealing that 45% of marriages in the country ultimately conclude in divorce. The divorce industry, with its array of lawyers, mediators, counselors, and more, has thrived, accumulating an estimated value exceeding 50 billion dollars in 2014 alone.

While these statistics are indeed striking, they do not capture the intentions with which individuals enter marriage. Nearly all individuals who marry (94%) express their aspiration to select an ideal partner, one who promises security, stability, endurance, and fulfillment throughout their shared journey. People embark upon this lifelong commitment with optimism and elevated expectations, hoping to weather life's trials together. However, the concept of marriage has evolved considerably in recent years. Marital relationships today are increasingly seen as voluntary commitments and expressions of love between two individuals. In some societies, this perspective has expanded to encompass all genders, further emphasizing the role of satisfaction and emotional fulfillment within partnerships.

Drawing from my pastoral experience, I have had the privilege of preparing and officiating numerous marriage ceremonies. These joyous occasions not only unite the bride and groom but also foster a sense of community as they celebrate the formation of new families. Nevertheless, alongside these moments of happiness, I have also borne witness to the painful journeys of many couples grappling with the challenges within their relationships. Unfortunately, for a significant number of these couples, divorce becomes the ultimate outcome. Studies have shown that couples often seek help only when the problems they face have been simmering beneath the surface for years, and the emotional toll runs deep. Traditionally, most research on divorce has focused on young couples and their specific circumstances, such as immaturity and lack of experience, as many divorces occur within the first three years of marital life.

Historically, the primary cause of marital dissolution was the death of a spouse. However, over the last two decades, the United States has witnessed a significant shift in this regard. Today, there are more divorced individuals than widowed, signifying that divorce has become the most frequent cause of marital dissolution. Between 1990 and 2010, the number of divorces among people aged 50 and older doubled in men and tripled in women, underscoring the evolving dynamics of marriage and divorce across generations.

The repercussions of divorce extend far beyond the dissolution of a marriage; they ripple through various aspects of individuals' lives and society. The negative consequences are multifaceted, impacting the health, finances, and education of those involved, as well as social cohesion, family stability, and even contributing to societal violence resulting from disintegrated families. For many, the fear of committing to another marriage lingers, affecting future relationships and decisions. These consequences have far-reaching implications, touching upon numerous areas of life.

For instance, a longitudinal study revealed that divorced individuals reported significantly lower life satisfaction and higher rates of depression compared to those in stable marriages. The impact of divorce transcends the dissolution of a legal contract; it profoundly influences the emotional and psychological well-being of those involved.

As we delve further into the complexities of marriage and divorce, this book aims to shed light on the evolving landscape of this institution, examining the motivations, challenges, and consequences that shape the lives of countless individuals and the broader society. Through stories, research, and insights, we will navigate the intricate tapestry of love, commitment, and the ever-changing dynamics of marriage in the modern world.

In our exploration of the evolving landscape of marriage and divorce, we must delve deeper into the complex factors contributing to the unraveling of marital bonds. While love remains the driving force behind many unions, numerous challenges and shifting societal dynamics have reshaped the modern marriage experience.

One such challenge lies in the changing nature of work and career aspirations. In the past, traditional gender roles often dictated that one partner would prioritize their career while the other managed the household and cared for the family. However, with the rise of gender equality and women's empowerment, modern couples face new dilemmas in balancing their professional and personal lives. Dual-career households are now the norm, placing added strain on couples as they juggle the demands of work and family.

Technology has also ushered in a new era of connectivity and communication. While it has brought people closer in some ways, it has also introduced a host of new challenges. The digital age has given rise to issues of infidelity and trust as social media, and dating apps make it easier to connect with potential romantic interests outside of marriage. The blurring lines between the online and offline worlds have created a complex landscape where boundaries are not always clear.

Moreover, our modern consumer culture has conditioned us to seek instant gratification and constant novelty. This mentality can seep into our relationships, making it challenging to weather the inevitable storms that come with long-term commitment. When difficulties arise, some individuals may be quick to consider divorce to escape the discomfort rather than work through the issues.

It's essential to acknowledge the impact of societal pressures and external influences on the perception of marriage. The media often glamorizes the idea of perfect, fairytale marriages, setting unrealistic expectations that can lead to disillusionment when reality falls short. Furthermore, the stigma once associated with divorce has diminished, making it a more socially acceptable option for couples facing difficulties.

The changing dynamics of family structures also play a significant role in how couples navigate their relationships. Blended families, where one or both partners have children from previous marriages, introduce additional complexities. These families must navigate the delicate balance of co-parenting, step-parenting, and the challenges of blending different family cultures and traditions.

Additionally, as people marry later in life or choose to remain single longer, they may bring with them a greater sense of independence and individualism. This can impact how they approach marriage, with some individuals prioritizing their personal growth and autonomy above all else.

Despite these challenges, it's important to remember that marriage is not solely defined by its difficulties and divorce rates. Many couples successfully navigate these obstacles, finding ways to strengthen their bonds and grow together. This book will explore the strategies, insights, and stories of resilience that shed light on the enduring power of love and commitment within the context of modern marriage.

Through a comprehensive examination of these complexities and the experiences of those who have traversed the intricate path of marriage and divorce, we aim to provide a holistic understanding of the forces at play in shaping the lives of individuals and the fabric of society itself. As we continue our journey through the ever-evolving landscape of marriage, we'll seek to uncover the secrets to lasting love, the art of compromise, and the ways in which couples can thrive in an era of unprecedented change and choice.

Social sciences have dedicated themselves to studying marital satisfaction to understand the reasons behind so many divorces. This research has mobilized great thinkers across various schools of thought and orientations. Despite this diversity, the debate on marriage remains relevant, given its centrality in people's lives and society. The benefits of a stable and prosperous marriage extend to all aspects of life. Many interventions in the form of marital therapies have been developed to help couples with issues. There are local, state, and federal programs to support marriage and the family. However, the divorce rate remains very high (45%). Numerous books have been published to help couples experience a good marital life. Courses and workshops on related topics are offered. Religions have premarital preparation programs. Society is aware of the importance of marriage, as well as the challenges and pain that accompany each divorce. But the desired results are far from being achieved. Against this backdrop, I attempt through this book to contribute to the current severe debate on the fundamental institution of human society: marriage.

TABLE OF CONTENTS

INTRODUCTION

Marriage, the timeless institution that binds hearts and lives together, is a tapestry woven with threads of universality and antiquity. It transcends cultures, races, and continents, reaching into the depths of human history. This sacred bond has stood the test of time, enduring through the ages as a testament to the profound connections between individuals.

UNIVERSALITY

Marriage is the common thread that weaves its way through the tapestry of humanity. Across the globe, people of diverse backgrounds unite in marriage, though the customs may vary. Recent advancements, such as the recognition of same-sex marriages in some countries, have expanded the boundaries of this ancient institution. However, with change comes complexity, as these shifts raise new questions and challenges within families. Regardless of the path taken, every culture and people recognize the essence of marriage. It is a cornerstone of society, built upon foundational principles and safeguarded by protective laws. To understand marriage is to delve into the very origins of life itself, for there was always a first union, and countless others followed.

ANTIQUITY

The origins of marriage are shrouded in the mists of time, a riddle that even the wisest among us cannot decipher.

Sacred texts, like the Bible, speak of Adam and Eve as the first couple, chosen by divine providence. Yet, in every corner of the world, myths and legends emerge to explain the inexplicable, to give meaning to the ineffable. These stories become the genesis of traditions passed down through generations, justifying the sacredness of marriage. It is a venerable institution as ancient as humankind itself.

THE SACREDNESS OF MARRIAGE

Marriage is no child's play; it is a profound commitment imbued with sacredness. Even the innocent games of children, mimicking couples or pretending to be parents, are swiftly met with the watchful eyes of society. The sanctity of marriage is reinforced by the protective mantle of law, making its dissolution a solemn and challenging process. What marriage entails is accepted as a given, unchallenged and unbroken. This reverence extends to the very symbols and components of marriage, such as the marital bed, a sacred space reserved solely for the union of spouses. With the blessings of priests, shamans, or elders, marriage transcends the realm of mere mortals, inviting the divine into its midst.

VULNERABILITY

As human as the very essence of marriage itself, vulnerability lurks in the shadows. It is a fragility that even the slightest issue can shatter, as evidenced by the rising number of divorces worldwide. In bygone eras, marriages endured for a lifetime, but today, those celebrating a decade together are hailed as heroes. Marriage is vulnerable not only to the differences between partners but also to external factors—poverty, ignorance, systemic pressures—that can test its strength. It can fall ill, suffering from discord, physical and emotional distance, ideological clashes, religious differences, and even diseases.

BEYOND COEXISTENCE

Mere cohabitation does not make up a valid marriage. Some couples, initially bound by love, see that love dwindles over time until indifference settles in. This book embarks on a journey to explore the intricate ingredients that make up the essence of marital relationships. Marriage is a nexus of life-generating interactions, a shared commitment to a family project so resolute that life's trials cannot tear it asunder. It is the symbol of unity. Whether living under the same roof or separated by circumstance, spouses feel the warmth of togetherness.

THE PROCESS OF UNION

The celebration of marriage is a process, a journey that weaves through various stages. It commences with the budding connection between two souls born from chance encounters, friendships, courtships, and engagements. Families from both sides come together, forging bonds and supporting their children's union. Society formalizes this union through civil and religious ceremonies, signifying the creation of a new family. Marriage is not a private affair; it requires the approval and recognition of many, culminating in a community celebration that acknowledges the ongoing cycle of life.

COURTSHIP AND FRIENDSHIP

Courtship is the initial stage where two individuals draw closer to each other, their connection growing through a series of events. It is marked by visits to each other's homes, where love blossoms quietly. In many cultures, it is the man who formalizes the conclusion of courtship, becoming a candidate for marriage sealing the commitment. Friendship plays a pivotal role, a stage often overlooked by some couples who rush into marriage, missing the opportunity to establish a strong foundation. True friendship, forged in loyalty, interest, and mutual support, paves the way for a lasting marital relationship.

THE CELEBRATION

In Western societies, the journey culminates with the grand wedding ceremony, preceded by festivities like bachelor and bachelorette parties. In contrast, some African cultures celebrate marriage multiple times, each ceremony spanning days, symbolizing the depth of their commitment.

MARITAL LIFE

With the official procedures complete, the couple embarks on a life together. They learn to understand each other better, sharing moments of joy and sorrow. But we'll delve deeper into this later in the book. Now, let's turn our attention to the twenty essential ingredients that compose the recipe for a successful marriage. Success in marriage is a subjective experience gauged by the level of satisfaction reported by the spouses. As we navigate this journey together, we'll explore ingredients drawn from pastoral, professional, and academic experiences. Our goal is to guide marriages toward fulfilling their mission of uniting two individuals in a meaningful family project, multiplying life, and realizing their aspirations.

A TIME OF CRISIS

Marriage, the bedrock of human society, faces unprecedented challenges in our time. It is my fervent hope that all marriages, regardless of culture or religion, can thrive. This book seeks to provide guidance to those who may have overlooked these ingredients and to couples preparing for their journey. These pages may also offer insights to those who have experienced the pain of divorce, shedding light on their past and helping them embark on new relationships with greater understanding and wisdom.

The structure of this book is straightforward. We will explore the meaning of each ingredient, supported by examples, and provide practical suggestions akin to a recipe for a successful marriage. As we conclude this journey, we shall approach the reality of marriage with humility and respect, cherishing the enduring institution that is marriage.

NAVIGATING THE INTRICATE TERRAIN OF IN-LAWS

The intricate dance with in-laws forms a foundational pillar in the societal and cultural edifice globally. Marriage is not merely a union of two hearts but a complex interplay between three distinct familial entities: the families of each partner and the nascent family they create together. In this delicate balance, in-laws wield considerable sway, each partner importing fragments of their familial heritage into the evolving tapestry of their shared life. Individuals often maneuver through their marital journey by either mirroring or intentionally deviating from the matrimonial blueprints sketched out by their progenitors.

The quintessential goal of matrimony is to forge a novel, sovereign family entity. However, achieving this autonomy frequently sparks a certain degree of tension, teetering between the yearning to break free from ancestral ties and the intrinsic craving for familial bonds. Consequently, not just the couple but their extended kin must make pivotal adjustments. The quest for a symphonic equilibrium becomes a critical factor in sculpting a marriage that is not just sustainable but also deeply fulfilling. Studies underscore the influential roles that in-laws and siblings-in-law play in the tapestry of marital satisfaction and quality.

Crafting a balanced dynamic within this emergent family structure often demands a reevaluation and recalibration of existing relationships. For instance, a father-in-law accustomed to his Sunday golf with his son might need to understand the couple's need for privacy or their own weekend plans. A well-meaning mother-in-law might inadvertently encroach by dispensing continuous advice, potentially breeding feelings of exasperation within the couple. She might insist on a particular way to organize the kitchen or critique their choice of decor, unintentionally causing friction. Conversely, in-laws can also emerge as pillars of unwavering support, and repositories of wisdom, such as when a sister-in-law shares her favorite family recipes or a brother-in-law helps with a DIY home project. However, the couple must foster a prudent distance from both sets of parents and relatives, as excessive involvement can beckon undue interference, threatening the very fabric of the marital bond.

The physical and symbolic realms should ideally echo the distinctive character of the three interwoven familial units. When a couple chooses to cohabit with one set of parents, an elevated level of maturity and unambiguous communication becomes vital to avert potential clashes. Perhaps the couple and the in-laws disagree on something as mundane as the weekly shopping list or TV volume, requiring negotiation and compromise. Moreover, interactions with siblings-in-law carry substantial weight. Instances may arise where a brother-in-law might make offhand comments about the couple's lifestyle choices, testing their patience and diplomacy.

Consider a scenario where a couple, endeavoring to enhance relations with their in-laws, embarks on regular family dinners. Though initiated with the best of intentions, disparities in culinary preferences or political ideologies might stir discomfort or discord. Perhaps one side of the family prefers a meat-heavy diet while the other is vegetarian, or political discussions at the table become too heated. The couple may need to devise strategies to bridge these differences, perhaps by instituting new traditions or subtly redirecting discussions away from polarizing subjects.

In the realm of holiday traditions, a couple might confront vastly divergent familial customs. One clan might revel in a lavish feast teeming with guests, while the other opts for a tranquil, introspective celebration. The couple might need to navigate these differences, perhaps dealing with a mother-in-law who expects her holiday pie to be the centerpiece or a father-in-law who insists on a particular type of tree. They might oscillate between attending each family's festivities, hosting their own amalgamated observance, or even forging new traditions that encapsulate the essence of their unique partnership.

This intricate web of relationships extends to the broader kin network, where a new spouse might find themselves navigating an intricate maze of expectations and social norms during extensive family congregations. In these scenarios, robust communication and mutual support within the couple are paramount, ensuring that neither partner feels isolated nor overwhelmed. Perhaps during a large family gathering, a new family member feels lost amidst the numerous aunts, uncles, and cousins, relying on their partner to introduce and integrate them into the fold.

Fostering positive relationships with in-laws and the extended family is pivotal for the couple's collective well-being and the vitality of their marriage. It necessitates a conscious endeavor to comprehend and honor the myriad family cultures without bias. Adopting a posture of acceptance and respect is crucial. For instance, a son-in-law might opt for engaging in respectful discourse rather than confrontation over disparate political views with his father-in-law. Similarly, a daughter-in-law might approach her sister-in-law's unique approach to parenting with a spirit of support rather than critique. In this intricate ballet of relationships, each step, each gesture towards understanding and respect, fortifies the bonds that shape the rich tapestry of family life.

This ethos of understanding, respect, and acceptance lays the foundation for the new family's growth and happiness. Getting to know each other's families well during the engagement and early marriage can significantly contribute to a harmonious life together. It's about striking a delicate balance between honoring the past and nurturing the present, ensuring that the new family unit not only survives but thrives while maintaining positive ties to its roots. This ongoing negotiation and adaptation are what ultimately define the successful integration into a new family through marriage, paving the way for generations of unity and understanding.

COMMUNICATION

Communication stands as the linchpin of spousal interaction, the very engine propelling the dynamics of marriage. It's through this intricate dance of dialogue and understanding that spouses gauge the health and depth of their union. At its core, communication serves as a conduit for information exchange, a shared exercise where the paramount goal for each participant is clarity and mutual comprehension. The philosophy of marriage communication springs from a vital principle, one reiterated throughout this book: marriage is a team endeavor with no victors or vanquished. Even amidst the most heated debates, communication must maintain a positive and constructive tone.

Two pivotal movements underpin the existence of healthy communication. Initially, the speaker must articulate their thoughts with precision and transparency. Countless marital spats stem from the erroneous belief that one's partner possesses mind-reading capabilities. It's a ludicrous expectation unsupported by any culture, law, or religious doctrine. Clarity, simplicity, and honesty mark the first step toward fostering meaningful exchanges. Post-expression, the second critical movement is verification. To circumvent misinterpretations, the listener must echo what they've understood, seeking confirmation. This simple act often defuses potential conflicts borne from defensive postures.

In numerous marital contexts, conversations are tinged with accusatory undertones and sweeping generalizations, which inevitably trigger defensive reactions. When one feels under attack and gears up for defense, they cease to listen, sparking a vicious cycle of miscommunication. Spouses often declare, "We've discussed this ad nauseam," while the other contends the opposite. Likely, the issue was broached, but neither party truly listened. Courtship often enjoys a more efficient communication channel, which, post-nuptials, seems to fray as life's complexities amass. To file baseless accusations or to indict without just cause is universally acknowledged as unfair. Yet, this is the trap of poor communication—expressing extreme sentiments over minor lapses, like a forgotten errand.

The caliber of communication can either be a marriage's balm or its poison, its salvation or its demise. While numerous couples diligently cultivate respect and constructive communication methods, others gradually desensitize, allowing the vital thread of dialogue to fray. Disagreements and differing opinions need not devolve into verbal skirmishes. Amidst the conflict, communication often suffers the most. Yet, as this book will further explore, communication is the cornerstone of a fulfilling marital journey. Whether it's navigating disagreements, discussing finances, parenting, planning leisure, or sharing affection, every aspect of coupledom is inextricably linked to communication. It's imperative, therefore, that spouses identify and continually refine their communication style, recognizing that effective dialogue is the result of concerted teamwork, not mere happenstance.

Building on the critical role of communication in matrimony, it's essential to acknowledge that effective dialogue is a cultivated art, not a spontaneous occurrence.

Active listening stands as a cornerstone of this art. It involves a complete immersion in the speaker's words an attentive silence where the focus is on understanding rather than responding. Another crucial facet is empathy. To communicate with empathy is to see through your partner's eyes, to grasp the emotions underpinning their words. Such understanding can significantly diminish conflicts and misunderstandings.

Non-verbal cues also play a pivotal role. Often, our deepest sentiments are conveyed not through words but through the subtleties of body language, facial expressions, and tone. Conversely, negative non-verbal like sarcastic tones or dismissive gestures can undermine even the most well-intentioned words. In conflict, establishing 'fair fight' rules—eschewing personal attacks and focusing on the issue at hand—is critical. It's about resolving the problem together, not emerging as the victor.

Regular emotional check-ins further fortify the communication bridge. Setting aside moments not just for logistical discussions but for sharing dreams, fears, and triumphs keeps the conversational current flowing strong. When communication falters, recognizing the need for external guidance, like a therapist or counselor, can be invaluable.

In summation, communication in marriage is a continuous journey of discovery, empathy, and connection. It's about forging a bond where both partners feel seen, heard, and cherished. While challenging, the fruits of a robust, communicative relationship are immeasurably rewarding. As you navigate life's shared path, let practical communication guide you, not as a mere tool but as the very essence of your union. In this journey, let every word, gesture, and silence between you be a testament to a love that speaks, listens, and resonates with profound understanding and respect.

CONFLICTS RESOLUTION

Differences in opinion, style, or feelings are part of the interaction within a couple. These differences create conflicts that the marriage must face and solve. For instance, consider Sarah and Tom, who regularly argue over how to discipline their children. Sarah believes in a more lenient approach, while Tom insists on stricter rules. The areas that generate the most problems are communication style, personal habits, finances, child-rearing, sexual intimacy, and the distribution of responsibilities within the home, like when Mike and Linda, who have different spending habits, end up in heated discussions over their monthly budget and expenses. In this book, these causes of conflict that I just mentioned are presented as ingredients for a fulfilling marriage. Anyone who has ever cooked knows that a poorly used ingredient can ruin any dish, much like how Julia felt when her partner, Mark, disregarded her ideas during a home renovation project, leading to resentment.

Scientific research has shown that conflicts can cause anxiety, sadness, depression, aggression, anger, resentment, and even hatred. Nearly all divorces are the outcome of some unresolved conflict. For example, Alex and Jamie's constant bickering over trivial matters escalated over time, leading to their separation. Conflicts lead to a distancing between the couple or an aggressive and abusive approach. I would like to pause here to clarify that violence and aggression are not solely the acts of men. Often, a woman can be, with her words or attitudes, the primary perpetrator of domestic violence. This matter deserves a whole separate book.

Conflict, considered as the result of diverging opinions or judgments, is inevitable in marital cohabitation. Conflict itself is neutral. The positive or negative effect of conflict on marital satisfaction depends on how the spouses resolve it. For example, when Emma and Jack disagree on vacation plans, they use it as an opportunity to explore new destinations together, turning a potential argument into a bonding experience. Before presenting the principles that enable good conflict resolution, it's important to point out that each spouse must know themselves. Like Rachel, who realized her tendency to withdraw in arguments wasn't helping and began working on expressing her feelings more openly. I will talk more about this when we get to ingredient number 20. Here, I would like to mention the importance of knowing how to handle emotions in the face of differing opinions. What is your reaction when you are angry? The most common responses to anger and conflict are open aggression, passive aggression, and passivity. In some people, anger causes behavioral disorders. They do and say things that are not consistent with their way of being or what they really want. For example, the woman who laments her husband's absence, whom she threw out of the house after an argument because, at that precise moment, she was furious. Like when Emily regretted harshly criticizing her husband, Ethan, in the heat of the moment. Some people maintain their composure when they are upset and look for ways to solve the conflict calmly. Knowing oneself helps to establish personal strategies toward conflict resolution. This self-awareness creates stability in the response and a certain predictability.

The next step after self-knowledge is openness to your partner. It's essential to have standard rules for conflict resolution. These rules are established in moments of peace and harmony. Many couples fail to resolve even the most minor conflicts because they lack resolution strategies. I know of a couple who had a big fight because they couldn't agree on the brand of cat food. Regardless of the nature of the conflict, the philosophy for good resolution, I insist, is always based on teamwork. The couple is a team, and the final outcome of each situation applies to the entire team, not just one of the two. The team loses, or the team wins. Working together means that each of the spouses has to abandon the project of being right. The desire or urge to be right is, in many cases, the biggest obstacle to the healthy resolution of problems because it stops being a team effort. When Kevin insisted, he knew the best way to fix the sink, ignoring his wife's suggestions, leading to more frustration and a still-broken sink. Putting aside who is right and working as a team is a sign of humility and maturity. Marriage is not child's play, as I already mentioned at the beginning. Adults have the capacity for discernment and can evaluate their goals and desires.

The desired outcome on the other side of any conflict is the return of harmony to the home. It's, therefore, crucial that the couple does not lose sight of this objective. Despite the fact that some emotions can heat up the discussion, the final prize should not be lost sight of. Every conflict well resolved strengthens the sentimental and emotional bonds between the couple and creates a better atmosphere within the family. Since the suffering of one of the spouses negatively affects the other, there's no need to "crucify" each other. After all, they are husband and wife, like when Nathan apologized to Claire after realizing his harsh words had hurt her deeply, and they worked together to find a solution.

Conflict resolution is achieved when both spouses seek a point of convergence. This approach is necessary to promote constructive dialogue between the two. That's why it's not recommended to try to resolve a conflict when tempers are flaring. It's necessary to wait for the appropriate moment. There is a broad consensus in affirming that conflict is not resolved amidst shouting. One might then ask what the point of shouting is. Some marriages would have perfect results in the shouting Olympics. They shout about everything all the time. If mothers knew that sometimes children laugh secretly when they are being shouted at, they would indeed feel ridiculous and might shout more than the tamale vendors of Mexico City or change their strategy. Amid shouting, no one listens, not even the person who is shouting. Keeping calm and looking for the best strategy to resolve the problem is a good ingredient for a fulfilling marriage. It's absolutely imperative to identify the conflict, its cause, and its effects on marital life.

Furthermore, it's not necessary to examine the family tree of the husband or wife to deduce that their great-grandfather, grandfather, and father were abusers of their wives. It's also not constructive to try to explain things with genetics. The conflict of the moment is not related to the DNA of the spouses, even though someone is repeating a behavior they saw in their family of origin. If the husband forgets the anniversary date of their wedding, this is not because his uncle suffers from amnesia.

The resolution of the conflict goes through exploring all workable solutions. Extreme options are eliminated to build a consensus that should be a new possibility, not what one person proposed. In cases where the husband defends his right to command from his subjectivity of "macho," marital satisfaction ends up being low or negative. One should never forget that the result is for the whole team. If the husband takes his wife fishing on the day she had breakfast with her friends, neither of them will likely enjoy that day. Conflict resolution requires openness on their part and mutual trust. A resolved conflict fosters a closer, intimate, and emotional approach. Humility works miracles in many cases. Recognizing one's mistakes and apologizing to one's partner are attitudes that resolve 90% of the conflicts in marital life. When there are many options to resolve a conflict, the spouses should be open to more than one negotiation session. It's not healthy to rush to seek external help at the precise moment of the conflict. The marital union has the privilege and potential for internal maintenance. Resolving a conflict is, precisely, practicing self-maintenance.

It's essential to recognize that each conflict, while potentially disruptive, also offers an opportunity for growth and more profound understanding between partners. Effective communication is the cornerstone of resolving these issues. Both partners must be willing to listen actively and empathize with the other's perspective. This doesn't mean simply waiting for your turn to speak but genuinely trying to understand the feelings and thoughts behind your partner's words, for when Henry took the time to understand why his wife, Maria, was upset about him working late again, leading to a constructive conversation about balancing work and family time.

Beyond active listening, expressing oneself clearly and respectfully is vital. Using "I" statements helps to own your feelings and reduce defensiveness from your partner. For example, saying, "I feel upset when the dishes aren't done," is more conducive to a positive discussion than "You never do the dishes." Such communication strategies prevent the escalation of conflict and promote a more constructive dialogue. When Lisa explained to her husband, Steve, how she felt overwhelmed with household chores and needed more help, leading to a fairer distribution of tasks.

Couples should also be aware of the importance of timing. Discussing a heated issue in the heat of the moment often leads to regrettable words and actions. Instead, it's sometimes better to take a brief time out to cool down and collect thoughts. This pause allows both partners to approach the conflict with a calmer, more rational mindset. For instance, when Olivia and Ethan decided to discuss their disagreement over holiday plans after a cooling-off period, they were able to reach a compromise without further conflict.

Moreover, understanding and respecting differences is crucial. Each person comes into a marriage with their unique background, beliefs, and ways of thinking. These differences needn't be obstacles; instead, they can enrich the relationship if approached with respect and curiosity. Seeking to understand your partner's point of view can reveal new insights and lead to compromises that satisfy both parties, like when Amit learned to appreciate the cultural traditions that were important to his wife, Leila, which brought them closer together.

Setting and respecting boundaries is another critical aspect of conflict resolution. Each person has their limits and comfort zones, and a healthy relationship needs to recognize and respect these. Boundaries can relate to personal space, how to manage finances, family interactions, and more. Discussing and agreeing on these limits can prevent many conflicts from arising. For example, when Grace and Noah agreed on a budget for their leisure activities, it helped prevent future arguments over spending.

Sometimes, despite the best efforts of both partners, conflicts can remain unresolved and continue to cause pain and frustration. In such cases, seeking the help of a marriage counselor or therapist can be a wise decision. A professional can supply a neutral perspective and guide couples through the process of understanding each other better and working through their issues. When Sophie and Ben, who were struggling with repeated arguments, sought counseling and learned new ways to communicate and understand each other's perspectives.

In the end, it's important to remember that conflict in marriage is normal and, when handled constructively, can lead to a stronger, more resilient relationship. The goal isn't to eliminate conflict entirely but to learn how to navigate it effectively. By understanding oneself, communicating effectively, respecting differences, and being willing to compromise and forgive, couples can resolve conflicts in a way that strengthens their bond and deepens their love and respect for each other. This process isn't always easy, but the rewards of a stable, loving marriage are well worth the effort.

EDUCATION

Throughout history, the concept of education has been closely tied to the expected roles individuals play within their families and societies. This relationship has been particularly pronounced when examining the differing educational paths prescribed for men and women across various cultures. Traditionally, men were encouraged to pursue education as a means to become providers and leaders within their communities. This role was seen as essential, and educational systems were designed to prepare men for their future responsibilities in governance and economic support of their families.

Conversely, the education provided to women was often limited and heavily influenced by the prevailing belief that their primary roles were to be homemakers and educators of the next generation. In many societies, a woman's worth was measured by her ability to support a household, raise children, and tend to her husband's needs. Some cultures even went as far as to dictate that the essence of a good wife lay in her submissiveness and unwavering support of her husband, who was often viewed as the unquestioned head of the household.

However, as the global society has evolved, so too have these archaic notions of gender-specific education. In recent years, there has been a significant shift towards more equal educational opportunities for all, regardless of gender. More girls and women are attending schools and universities, leading to a workforce where women stand shoulder-to-shoulder with men across a vast array of professions. This evolution in education has brought about significant changes in traditional familial and societal roles.

The impact of increased education levels among both men and women has been profound. Studies have consistently shown that when both spouses are educated, the quality of the marriage tends to improve. Higher levels of education lead to better communication, as individuals are more confident and articulate in expressing their thoughts and feelings. This, in turn, fosters a greater sense of mutual respect and understanding. Moreover, as both partners often contribute financially to the household, a new dynamic of equality and partnership replaces the outdated provider-dependent model.

Despite these advancements, resistance to change persists in some quarters. Some men view educated women as a challenge to their traditional authority and may resist or undermine their partners' educational aspirations. Conversely, some women may use their education as a platform to assert themselves in their relationships, challenging the traditional power dynamics. This can sometimes lead to competitiveness between spouses, overshadowing the many positive aspects of a dual-education household.

Yet, the overarching narrative is still one of progress and empowerment. Education is universally acknowledged as a valuable asset in an individual's life, enriching their understanding of the world and enhancing their ability to make informed decisions. Even in households where one partner chooses to stay at home, the level of education that person has received can significantly affect their effectiveness and satisfaction in their role.

Education's influence extends beyond the household and into broader society. As more individuals, particularly women, achieve higher levels of education, they increasingly take part in civic and community activities. They are better equipped to understand and advocate for health and wellness, and they play a crucial role in promoting the education of their children, thereby perpetuating a cycle of learning and empowerment.

However, the journey towards genuinely fair access to education and the dismantling of gender stereotypes is far from complete. In many regions of the world, cultural norms and systemic barriers continue to limit educational opportunities, particularly for women and girls. Overcoming these challenges requires a multifaceted approach, including policy reform, community engagement, and a continued emphasis on the intrinsic value of education for all individuals.

The advent of technology, particularly the rise of online learning, has played a transformative role in making education more accessible. With a plethora of courses and resources available at their fingertips, individuals can now pursue a wide range of subjects and skills, regardless of their geographical location or socio-economic status. This democratization of knowledge has the potential to level the playing field and open new horizons for millions worldwide.

In a world grappling with complex and interrelated challenges such as climate change, economic instability, and global health issues, the importance of a well-educated populace cannot be overstated. Educated individuals are better prepared to understand these challenges, think critically, and devise innovative solutions. They are also more adaptable and able to navigate the rapidly changing landscape of the modern world.

In conclusion, while significant strides have been made towards achieving a more equitable and enlightened society through education, the journey is ongoing. The transformative power of education remains a beacon of hope and a fundamental tool for empowerment, understanding, and growth. As societies continue to evolve and embrace the value of education for all, the vision of a world where every individual has the opportunity to thrive and contribute meaningfully seems increasingly within reach.

EMPLOYMENT

There's no doubt that today's employment situation impacts a couple's life. Here, I address the topic of one or both members' employment as an ingredient for greater marital satisfaction. I would like to start with a brief historical overview of the evolution of employment within family life. Before the 19th-century Industrial Revolution, all family members had to work for subsistence. After this era, legislation was introduced that separated wage work from housework. This was accompanied by the concept of public and private life. The vast majority of families adopted this model as a cultural prototype of family life by the mid-20th century. Essentially, it was understood that one member of the couple worked outside the home for a salary (generally the husband), and the other worked in the home without pay (generally the wife).

In the second half of the 20th century, the cultural paradigm regarding work and marital life changed again. Many women started working outside the home. This created a situation where there was no one at home to fully dedicate themselves to household needs. Nowadays, it is estimated that in 50% of couples, both work. With these numbers, it's clear that working outside the home plays an important role in the quality of the marital relationship.

The reality of employment today requires workers to spend many hours at work; hence, they spend more time at their jobs. There is greater work pressure and less time for cohabitation. Despite this stress, half of the couples prefer both to be in salaried jobs. However, the old mindset that the man is the provider and the woman the homemaker, even though she works outside the home, has not yet been eliminated. What can be done to make work an ingredient of marital satisfaction?

When both partners are employed, certain couples may find that there is added stress or strain placed on the woman in the relationship. Besides her job outside, she has to continue being a wife, mother, homemaker, and caretaker of others. Typically, workplaces outside the home do not help accommodate the woman in her multiple roles and responsibilities. This can be a source of anxiety and tension in the couple. For many women, this reality creates a limitation in their aspiration for professional development. For instance, in the private sector, it happens that a department director needs schedule flexibility from their employees according to the company's needs. This puts the woman in conflict. Sometimes, it's also required to stay later at work to handle an urgent matter.

The couple has to study their situation and adopt strategies that safeguard sufficient income without sacrificing the attention required in household work. In some cases, both spouses have to work. They spend a lot of time outside the house and arrive tired. In this situation, the distribution of household responsibilities should be more equitable and not overburden the woman. When both work, there's a sense of equality between them for several reasons. Both contribute to the family income, and each is developing professionally. These couples have better communication, less domination, and less anxiety. Episodes of jealousy, control, manipulation, and domestic violence are also reduced. Each member of the couple understands the demands of work and occupies their mind positively to fulfill their work tasks.

It has been observed that when both spouses work, there's greater confidence in interaction and cohabitation. The use of the phone, for example, does not create as many problems. It's understandable that nowadays, one can continue working by phone even when already at home. Employment of both also favors fidelity and emotional stability. Work outside the home consumes many energy resources. On arriving home, the spouses want to rest, and there's no time to look for better offers outside because the anxiety level at home is low.

In other situations, one member of the couple earns enough for the family to live well on a single income. Many of these couples live the traditional dynamic where the man is the provider, and the woman takes care of the house and children. It is important, however, that this arrangement is a common agreement. Although it's very positive for one of them to take care of the house and children when necessary, it doesn't have to be, by default, the woman. It's increasingly common for the woman to earn a better salary than the man. In such cases, she can work outside, and the husband can work at home. In modern culture, enough maturity is required on both sides so that, on the one hand, the woman doesn't fall into the presumption of wearing the "pants," and on the other, the man doesn't perceive himself in the "shameful" quality of being kept. They are work agreements between the couple.

I insist every light casts a shadow. When only one member of the couple works outside, care must be taken not to stop appreciating the role of both in-home well-being. Cases have been seen where the one who brings in the money perceives themselves as superior to the one who stays at home. Conversely, cases have also been seen where the one who stays at home blackmails the one who works outside. This can arise from a tantrum because one of them went to sleep early, spent a lot of time on the phone for work reasons, or because they traveled alone with their secretary for several days. When jealousy settles in a couple's relationship, the result is always disastrous. There's a lot of abuse, unnecessary "hits," and sure wounds. It's good not to lose sight of the fact that it's a blessing for both to be able to work when there's a need to do so.

Work is good for marital satisfaction. However, it has to be negotiated who works outside the home. When both decide to work outside, there's the option of hiring someone responsible for household chores, as well as postponing procreation. What's important is that the couple negotiates their choices and that the distribution of responsibilities is fair.

There's another important topic that can't be overlooked. Work requires a great emotional investment. Professionally, if someone wants to progress, they have to, so to speak, put their soul into the work. And although it may seem strange, also the work inside the home can take a great emotional toll. In the effort to do their job well for the family's sake, the spouses must be careful not to emotionally detach from each other to the extent of neglecting their marriage. I know a good number of cases where work transformed into poison for marital satisfaction, as it became an excuse not to cohabitate with the partner or was a cause of infidelities. For couples with university studies, the danger is in the lack of balance. They can focus so much on their professional growth that they leave the marital relationship in second place. Conversely, couples without great professional potential may fall into the other extreme, putting little effort into job success to live more intensely the marital cohabitation. Couples in this second situation sometimes live with their in-laws for more than ten years and feel happy. In my opinion, living with in-laws is not an ideal situation for life as a couple. It should only be an option in strictly necessary cases.

Living with in-laws, while sometimes necessary, can introduce additional dynamics that may impact the marital relationship. This living arrangement can sometimes lead to a lack of privacy and independence, which are crucial for nurturing a healthy and strong marriage. Moreover, it can create an environment where the couple becomes overly reliant on their extended family, potentially stifling their growth as a unit and as individuals. It's essential for couples in this situation to establish boundaries and maintain open communication with their in-laws to foster a harmonious living environment.

Additionally, it's worth considering the impact of cultural expectations on employment and marital satisfaction. In many cultures, there are deeply ingrained beliefs about the roles of men and women in the workforce and the home. These cultural norms can influence a couple's decisions and feelings about work and home life balance. It's important for couples to critically assess these cultural expectations and decide what works best for their relationship and individual well-being.

The rise of remote work and flexible working arrangements also plays a significant role in the modern employment-marital satisfaction equation. With more companies offering the option to work from home, couples have more opportunities to balance work and home responsibilities effectively. This shift can lead to reduced stress, more time for family, and better work-life balance. However, it also requires couples to be diligent about setting boundaries between work and personal life to prevent one from encroaching on the other.

Furthermore, the pursuit of career satisfaction and personal development shouldn't be overlooked. When individuals are fulfilled and satisfied in their professional lives, it often translates into a more positive attitude at home. Encouraging and supporting each other's career goals can strengthen the bond between partners, fostering mutual respect and understanding.

In conclusion, while employment is undeniably a critical factor in marital satisfaction, it's the approach and attitude towards work, the division of responsibilities, and the ability to adapt and communicate that truly determine its impact. As society continues to evolve, so too will the dynamics of work and marriage. It's up to each couple to navigate these waters in a way that brings them closer and ensures both their relationship and individual needs are met. Finding this balance is a continuous process, one that requires patience, understanding, and an unwavering commitment to each other's happiness and well-being.

CHILDREN

The birth of a baby remains, for more than 90% of people in most surveys, the culmination of love between spouses. Procreation is an essential function of marriage. Regardless of culture or religion, birth is considered a blessing. The presence of children gives direction and meaning to all family activities. Parents live and strive for their children.

Scientific research has shown that the presence of children reduces the likelihood of conflict between spouses and increases satisfaction with their marital relationship. Spouses put all their energy into their children and pay less attention to personal issues. I must say, and I will explain why I say it, that this same ingredient can alter the taste of the marital soup. Let me explain. Many spouses complain that since the birth of the children, they have taken a back seat in terms of the attention they expect to receive from their wives. The lady is so busy attending to her children that the husband is no longer a priority. This phenomenon is called triangulation. In human relationships where there are more than two parties, triangles tend to form with two positive sides and one negative side. It is common to see mothers and their children forming the positive sides of the triangle and becoming closer to each other. The husband or father is left out of this relationship as the negative side of the triangle. In many cases, spouses become closer again when the children enter adolescence. The rebellion of teenagers places them on the negative side of the triangle while the parents form a team to deal with the "monster" that has come to steal their boy or girl: adolescence.

There is no doubt that children change the dynamics of interaction between spouses. However, children are markers of times and seasons in their lives. Their arrival in the family helps them to appreciate the journey taken. The tasks inherent in their education point towards the future and determine the purpose of the parents' lives. As they grow up, children generate good and bad memories of their father's or mother's life. In an angry and tantrum-prone child, the father or mother may remember their own childhood. In the affectionate and responsible girl, one can relive that youth surrounded by the affection, tenderness, and support of the parents. I have had the opportunity to talk to many parents about their children. Our meeting generally begins with the search for advice to accompany a son or daughter who has become a real challenge and, in some cases, a tremendous headache. Interestingly, as we talk about their children, there is always a pride that cannot be hidden: many parents have confessed to me that their own mischief was greater than the trouble their children are now causing them.

Marriage is organized around children. In recent years, there has been a large number of divorces once the children leave home. But at the same time, it is common to hear couples openly declare that their marriage has been saved thanks to their children. It is natural for couples to strive to give the world children who are ready for success. This common goal demands real teamwork between the spouses and transforms into an extremely important ingredient for a good marital experience.

This teamwork in raising children often brings a deeper level of understanding and cooperation between spouses. They learn to navigate the complexities of life together, balancing their roles as parents and partners. This journey, albeit filled with challenges, also brings a myriad of joyous moments. From witnessing their child's first steps to celebrating academic and personal achievements, these events strengthen the bond between the couple, reminding them of their shared love and commitment.

Moreover, children serve as a mirror, reflecting aspects of each parent's personality and upbringing. This reflection can be enlightening, sometimes leading parents to introspect and grow personally. They may also recognize and appreciate their partner's qualities more as they see these traits passed down to their children. This cycle of mutual appreciation and growth can further solidify the marital relationship.

However, it's important to note that while children can enhance a marriage, they should not be the sole glue that holds a relationship together. A healthy marriage requires effort and nurturing beyond the realm of parenthood. Couples must ensure they invest time and energy in maintaining their romantic relationship, separate from their identity as parents. This involves regular communication, spending quality time together, and keeping the flame of romance alive.

In cases where children have grown and left home, parents often face the 'empty nest' syndrome. This phase can be a critical test for a marriage. For some, it's a time to rediscover each other and enjoy the freedom and quiet that comes with no children at home. For others, it can be a challenging period filled with feelings of loss and uncertainty about their role and identity. It is crucial for couples to prepare for and adapt to this new phase of life, finding new hobbies, interests, or goals to pursue together.

In conclusion, while children undoubtedly bring significant changes to a marriage, they also offer opportunities for growth, joy, and deeper connection. A successful marriage, in the context of parenting, is one where the couple continues to nurture their relationship alongside their journey as parents, adapting to each stage of life with resilience and mutual support.

FINANCES

I'll begin this chapter with some statistics that might surprise you. Nowadays, people invest over 75% of their time and energy working to earn money or thinking about money. Money is on people's minds more than other things, such as their relationships, sex, work, and health. There's no doubt that financial matters hold a significant place in marriage-related decisions, from the beginning to the end. When two young individuals are considering marriage, even when being in love is the official reason, there are other serious matters to consider, such as the economy and finances of the future couple. Parents want to ensure that their son or daughter won't be in a precarious situation as a result of the marriage. We might think infidelity and violence are the most common causes of divorce. However, surveys of divorced individuals indicate that half of the divorces are related to financial matters. Money is one of the biggest sources of tension and marital anxiety. Although it might seem strange, for some couples, talking about money is as taboo as talking about sex. It's also true that disagreements about finances are a consequence of other issues the couple is experiencing.

In every couple, there are arrangements and agreements, verbal and non-verbal, for managing finances. There's no one-size-fits-all formula. But the relationship that each person has with money and the place it holds in the dynamics of a couple's life is definitely determining elements of the quality of the marriage. Money means different things to different people. Some see it as a symbol of stability and peace, others as an instrument of power and control. I knew of a marriage where the wife earned more than $100,000 a year and the husband $55,000. He managed all the family's finances and gave her less than $100 a month for her expenses and those of their two children. The marriage ended in divorce after 12 years.

Many studies have shown that couples who have managed their finances well enjoy better marital satisfaction. It's not always a question of amount. Some couples have a lot of money but do not enjoy a good relationship. The secret is in the management. This is achieved when accounts are clear. There must be a budget for the household, and each member of the couple also deserves an allowance. It's always better to establish clear rules regarding financial matters. We must be responsible with payments and with balancing the accounts. It's also true that where there's no need for money, there's less tension and anxiety when it comes to meeting everyday needs. Couples who lack enough money for basic household functions experience difficulties in their communication and interaction.

In some cases, it's necessary for each individual to have their own bank account and for contributions to the family account to be well established. Many couples have problems because one of them is not transparent in managing money. Generally, the less transparent person is the one who wants to have control of the finances. No one denies that money contributes positively to marital satisfaction if the agreements are clear and respected. But as I mentioned earlier, a poorly used ingredient can also spoil the dish.

One of the challenges in terms of finances is the style of spending money. Discussions often start over the disagreement one partner has about the way the other spends money. This can be related to the ages at which people marry. Surveys indicate that the average age of marriage has increased. For men, in Western cultures, the average age is 28-30 years; for women, 25-28 years. At this age, generally, the individual is already working and managing their money without having to negotiate with someone else. One of the first adjustments once married is, precisely, money management. The man might like to use his salary to buy sports cars with all the new "toys" they come with. She might like exclusive brand handbags and fine jewelry. In marriage, each will have to adjust their tastes to the new reality. This also involves a new element: taking into account the opinion of their partner regarding money management.

Some of the challenges couples face today are debt and savings. Many young people already have debts when they get married. It could be student loans or credit cards. It's not very common to have savings. The beginning of the new family's life implies greater expenses, such as buying a house and furnishing it, not to mention, in some cases, the big wedding party. Merging debts and deciding on a payment strategy doesn't seem to be very difficult for young couples. The problem, according to surveys, seems to be in the way of saving. This problem can become more serious if one of the partners is at one of the common extremes: spending too much or not wanting to spend. There are people who tend to spend a lot on their personal tastes. There are others who feel uneasy if they don't have enough savings. Although one of them knows how to balance spending and saving, the extreme behavior of the other can cause problems.

The ease of access to credit has generated a series of new challenges in couples' financial policies. Historically, couples produced what they needed to survive and lived with what they produced. Nowadays, easy loans and credit cards mean that many couples spend more than they produce. It's like a vicious circle, a trap, or a difficult disease to cure. The system is organized in such a way that when the couple starts using credit, they sometimes end up trapped in a tunnel with no way out. Credit cards have high-interest rates, and it's hard to settle them. And even though they continue to pay every month, the continuous use of these cards means the couple continues to get into debt. The market culture presents having credit and debts as positive attributes. That's why, to buy any valuable item, you have to demonstrate a good credit history, which not only includes payment habits but also the age of credit use.

The task of each couple is to define the place that money occupies in their life. It's true that there are many things that money can buy, but each couple must have a list of what they plan to buy according to the amount of money they generate. However, they should not overlook also making a "list" of things that money can't buy, thus achieving a healthy balance. For example, money can't buy a man or a woman what they most need, such as feeling loved and respected. It's important, then, to know that money has reaches and limits. For finances to be a good ingredient for marital satisfaction, the couple must devise a realistic budget that includes proper debt management, as well as some savings.

This realistic budget and savings plan should not only cover current needs but also anticipate future challenges and opportunities. It's wise for couples to discuss and agree on short-term and long-term financial goals. These can range from saving for a vacation or a new car to planning for retirement or children's education. Regularly reviewing these goals and the progress made towards them can help keep both partners engaged and committed to their shared financial future.

In addition to setting goals, understanding each other's financial mindset is crucial. Often, individuals bring different attitudes and experiences related to money into a relationship. One may be a spender, enjoying the immediate pleasures that money can bring, while the other might be a saver, focusing on future security. These differences don't have to be divisive. Instead, they can offer balance, with each partner learning from the other's perspective. Open and honest communication about money, including the fears, challenges, and aspirations each person has, can strengthen the relationship and build a solid foundation for making joint financial decisions.

Furthermore, it's important for couples to educate themselves about financial matters. This can involve learning about budgeting, investments, insurance, and retirement planning. There are many resources available, from books and online courses to financial advisors. Investing time in education can pay significant dividends, helping couples make informed decisions that will benefit their financial future.

As couples navigate their financial journey, they should also be aware of the impact of external factors. Economic conditions can change, affecting jobs, investments, and the cost of living. Having a flexible approach, being willing to adapt plans, and having an emergency fund can help couples manage through uncertain times.

Additionally, couples should consider the legal and tax implications of their financial decisions. Understanding the benefits and responsibilities of joint accounts, the implications of buying property together, or how marriage affects taxes can prevent surprises and conflicts later on. Consulting with a financial advisor or a tax professional can provide valuable guidance tailored to a couple's specific situation.

Finally, it's important to remember that while money is a critical aspect of life, it's not the only one. Balancing financial goals with other priorities, such as spending quality time together, pursuing personal interests, and maintaining health and well-being, is crucial for a fulfilling life. Couples should strive to find harmony between their financial plans and the other elements that make their relationship and life together rich and rewarding.

In conclusion, managing finances as a couple is a complex but essential task. It involves more than just numbers; it's about understanding each other, setting shared goals, and making informed decisions together. By approaching financial management as a team, with open communication and a willingness to learn and adapt, couples can build not just a strong financial foundation but also a stronger, deeper relationship.

SEXUAL INTIMACY

Sexual relations can be considered as a measure of a couple's relationship health. Simply put, good sexual relations signal a stronger emotional connection between spouses. This act is the culmination of openness, trust, and mutual commitment. However, there are cases where sex is used as a distraction from addressing contentious issues. When one or both partners avoid discussing a sensitive topic, they might resort to sex to pretend everything is fine. Often, this is only a temporary fix as the problem doesn't get resolved simply through sexual intimacy. Similarly, some may use sex as a tool for manipulation to gain something or to control and dominate. Undoubtedly, the quality of sexual intimacy is directly linked to other aspects of the marital relationship, such as communication, conflict resolution, finances, leisure time, and parenting. Generally, a better emotional connection enjoys better sexual intimacy. Likewise, a couple in conflict rarely achieves satisfying sexual relations.

Many surveys indicate that two of the biggest challenges couples face regarding sexuality are discussing their sexual relationship and evaluating the affection they receive. Over time, signs of affection may wane, leading to routine, often becoming monotonous. Interestingly, even in couples married for over ten years, there's a lack of confidence when it comes to discussing their sexual practices. Many prefer to avoid the subject to prevent misinterpretations or insinuations.

Each partner evaluates the quality of their sexual intimacy based on the affection they receive. Definitions of affection vary greatly between genders. As I'll discuss in more detail in the chapter dedicated to gender differences, women prioritize affection before sex, while men perceive affection as a result of sexual intimacy. Generally, surveys indicate that happy couples also enjoy good sexual intimacy, as each partner feels satisfied with the amount of affection they receive. A wife is content with the expressions of affection from her husband, which don't always lead to sex. A husband is satisfied with the frequency of sexual relations with his wife, and all are happy. This isn't achieved magically or mechanically; it requires discussion and agreement.

The quality of sexual intimacy largely depends on communication between spouses. In some cases, one might feel their feelings are disregarded, and the other is only concerned with their needs. Poor communication often accompanies various complaints, for instance, about the frequency and style of sexuality. For some, twice a week might seem too much, while for others, it's almost never enough. It's important to understand that a couple's needs aren't always in sync. Synchronization is achieved through agreements. Studies show that men and women interpret the connection between sexual intimacy and the health of their marital relationship differently. For women, the state of the relationship precedes sexual desire. When a woman is upset with her husband over an incident, she has no sexual desire. For men, on the other hand, there's a separation between sexual intimacy and the relationship. After a heated argument, a man is still willing to engage in sexual relations with his wife.

Another point to consider regarding gender differences is the expression of affection. For women, a hug or caress may be enough to feel, receive, and respond to affection from their husbands. For men, generally, holding hands and caressing seem insufficient. As mentioned earlier, sensitivity to the other person's needs is crucial. It's not about satisfying just one's needs but both. Negotiation is mandatory, and this is achieved by discussing the topic. However, surveys and studies show that talking about sex is not easy among spouses. It's uncommon to receive education at home on how to discuss sexual matters, as these topics maintain a dimension of taboo. Each person builds their own understanding of the subject, with the potential to adopt erroneous ideas. Uncertainty about how to properly express their emotions and sexual desires means that many couples never broach the subject. Things happen mechanically, and a routine is established. But to achieve greater satisfaction in sexual intimacy, it's essential to discuss the topic.

Continuing the discussion, it's crucial to recognize the psychological and emotional components of sexual intimacy. The psychological well-being of each partner significantly influences their sexual relationship. Issues such as stress, anxiety, or depression can severely impact one's sexual desire and performance. Understanding and addressing these psychological factors is vital for a healthy sexual relationship. Partners need to be attentive to each other's mental health and offer support when needed. It's not just about physical satisfaction but also about emotional and psychological well-being.

Moreover, societal and cultural influences play a significant role in shaping individuals' attitudes and expectations regarding sexual intimacy. Cultural norms and beliefs can either positively or negatively impact one's perception and experience of sexual relations. Couples may come from different cultural backgrounds, leading to different expectations and beliefs about sex, which can cause misunderstandings and conflicts. Open and honest communication about these cultural differences is essential in finding common ground and building a mutually satisfying sexual relationship.

Furthermore, as couples age, they may experience changes in their sexual desires and capabilities. Physical changes due to aging, health issues, and medications can affect sexual function and desire. It's important for couples to understand and accept these changes as a natural part of life and adapt their sexual practices accordingly. They may need to explore new ways of expressing their sexuality and intimacy, focusing more on emotional connection, touch, and other forms of affection.

Education and counseling can also play a significant role in enhancing sexual intimacy. Many couples may benefit from sex education to better understand each other's bodies, responses, and needs. Sex therapists or counselors can provide guidance and strategies to improve communication, address specific sexual issues, and enhance the overall sexual experience.

In addition, building and maintaining a strong emotional bond outside the bedroom is crucial. Engaging in shared interests, spending quality time together, and showing appreciation and respect for each other contribute to a stronger emotional connection, which, in turn, can lead to a more fulfilling sexual relationship.

Lastly, it's essential to recognize that every couple is different, and what works for one may not work for another. There's no one-size-fits-all approach to sexual intimacy. Each couple needs to explore and find what works best for them, remaining receptive and ready to adjust and evolve. Regularly checking in with each other, discussing desires, concerns, and fantasies, and being willing to experiment and explore new things can keep the sexual relationship fresh and satisfying.

In conclusion, sexual intimacy is a complex and multifaceted aspect of a relationship that extends far beyond the physical act. It involves psychological, emotional, cultural, and physiological components. By understanding and addressing these factors, couples can build a deeper, more satisfying sexual connection that enhances their overall relationship and well-being.

THE AGREEMENTS

Agreements between spouses strengthen and increase marital satisfaction. There are two types of agreements: those that are part of life plans, that is, outside of a conflict situation, and agreements that are the result of a difference of opinion. The first category of agreements is of utmost importance in organizing coexistence as a couple. Studies indicate that these agreements carry more weight than all the rules that exist. Everyone first encounters this type of agreement in their family of origin. Living together requires a set of rules to achieve harmony and peace. Educating children includes learning about family agreements. Parents reach agreements on how to educate their children. Children learn what agreements are and the consequences of not respecting them. Reaching agreements and adhering to them is the first school of commitment and responsibility that every human being attends in the early years of their life. The child knows that the agreement is to get good grades and behave well if they want to continue enjoying their toys.

In married life, those who grew up in a family where agreements and their application were clearly discussed have an easier time negotiating with their partner. Those who grew up in a family under the tyranny of one of their parents often fear negotiating agreements. In families where there is machismo and domestic violence, children grow up with fear, and this fear is carried over into marital coexistence. The couple must base their discussions on agreements under the principle of equality. The goal is to create spaces where each person feels comfortable. No one is superior, and no one is always right. A good negotiation to reach solid agreements uses the same technique as communication. It's a three-step exercise. The first step is the clear expression of what each person wants. The second step is to listen and connect with the other person in their desire. The third and final step is to come to an arrangement that is fair for everyone. The various facets and events of a couple's life go through agreements. Experience shows that in the absence of prior and clear agreements, the result is chaotic and negative. For example, if the couple does not establish agreements on managing finances, it's difficult to balance income with expenses. The same applies to the education of children, the use of free time, and sexual intimacy.

The other time when it is necessary to reach constructive agreements is in the face of differences of opinion in the couple. Faced with a dilemma, for example, there are basically three options: that each person does what they want, that one of the two concedes, or that an agreement is reached. The key to negotiating agreements is, first of all, to abandon the individual project of being right. Marriage is between two people, not just one of them and their ideas. To be able to negotiate agreements with your partner, a person has to take a reality check. Those who are not willing to share decision-making with their partner will be happier staying single, and by the way, they will do us all a great favor. Marriage is necessarily a team effort. If spouses are not willing to make decisions together, they will have many unresolved conflicts and low marital satisfaction. Sometimes, you hear some spouses say with pride that they are the ones who make all the decisions in their house and that the other person is okay with it. In reality, there is no such conformity, as everyone wants their opinion to be taken into account. What is real is that frequently, it is one of the spouses who dominates or manipulates their partner. In other cases, one of them opts to be passive and not participate in decision-making. Working as a team means thinking about what is best for both of you. I insist marriage is for two.

Entering the negotiation requires an attitude of openness. As with good communication, knowing how to listen requires that you turn off your own inner radio and tune into your partner's channel. Listening means not worrying about the response to give. When someone is applying to negotiate over a difference, they have to step out of their own opinion for a moment to listen to the other. In some cases, by listening well, the person discovers that, in fact, there is no such difference of opinion. It takes time and practice to achieve synchronization and understand the other person's way of reasoning. Moreover, listening to the other requires not only this internal disposition but also appropriate body language, which varies according to culture. Some studies indicate that someone who listens with their arms crossed is closing themselves off and doesn't want to connect with the other person. But it's also true that in some cultures, crossing your arms is a sign of respect and attention. The essential point here is that both members of the couple must assure each other that they are entering the negotiation with open minds.

The other aspect of the attitude required to negotiate agreements between the couple is visualizing the final outcome. It's essential to remember that the final agreement may be different from your idea, preference, or expectation. This attitude directly connects with abandoning the eagerness to be right. The couple owe each other mutual respect. Each one thinks and has an opinion. It's sad to see that, in some cases, one of them adopts the stance that things should always be done their way. When this way of being is the standard, whims, tantrums, anxiety, anger, and resentment become the common denominator in the marital relationship, and the path to divorce is a high-speed highway.

There are some basic rules for all types of negotiation. It's essential to remember that the couple seeks harmony and peace. It's hard to conceive that someone enjoys being in conflict unless the person is mentally ill. The desired result for everyone is to reach a good agreement. Therefore, the tone of voice and the way to start the negotiation are key to the final resolution. If one of them attacks or criticizes, they will likely receive a defense, counterattack, or displeasure in response. If the tone of voice is brutal, the response will be another brutal tone of voice or shutdown, and there will be no negotiation, much less the desired result. Therefore, it's not advisable to negotiate agreements when someone is upset or in the middle of a heated discussion. It's necessary to wait for tempers to cool to connect with the other person. If couples forget a bit about their pride and tantrums, they have a great capacity to learn to calm each other down. But many times, they do not use this capacity to show weakness. At these moments, they forget that they are a team. The team wins, or the team loses. The final outcome affects everyone.

Negotiating means accepting that there are differences in preferences or opinions. In many cases, the couple focuses on these points of difference to find a solution. There's a very simple principle that we often forget. You cannot solve a problem from a position of weakness. If you're stuck in the mud up to your waist, it will be difficult and even impossible for you to pull another person who is also trapped to firm ground. It's necessary to be on firm ground to be able to help the other out. This principle means that problems are solved from a position of strength and not weakness. In a negotiation, the points of strength are those on which the couple agrees. It's from here that the negotiation begins. From this firm ground, it will be easier to pull the points of difference.

At the end of the negotiation, teamwork goes hand in hand with the flexibility of each member of the couple. As I mentioned earlier, openness to changing one's mind is required. You are married to your partner, not to your own ideas. Reaching an agreement is always the victory.

MUTUAL SUPPORT

Through numerous encounters with couples, I've had the privilege to witness the profound impact of mutual support on the quality of a marriage. Couples often speak of their experiences with mutual support as a source of immense pride and fulfillment. To cultivate this vital dimension of marital relationships, two essential elements come to the forefront: genuine interest in one's partner and unwavering respect.

First and foremost, the foundation of mutual support lies in demonstrating a sincere interest in your partner. During the courtship phase, many couples cite the significance of feeling genuinely cared for by their prospective life partners when deciding to embark on their marital journey together. To be interested means to manifest one's desire to truly understand and connect with the other person. Instances where this interest is lacking are regrettably common. It's unfortunate that some young men grow up with misguided notions about marriage. For instance, when a 17-year-old forbids his girlfriend from maintaining friendships outside the relationship, it raises a red flag for future support deficits. Similarly, when a young man asserts that his future wife need not work because he will be the sole provider, it sends another warning signal. True interest in one's partner extends to wanting to explore their desires and aspirations.

In many cases of marital strife that I've encountered, a significant portion of the resentment that women harbor toward their husbands after several years of marriage can be traced back to a lack of genuine interest. Many express regrets for abandoning their youthful dreams when they entered into their relationships. They lament not completing their education or discontinuing their careers. Some even admit that their partners discouraged them from pursuing further education, assuring them they wouldn't need to work. Two decades into their marriages, these women realize they failed to advocate for their dreams and resent that it's now seemingly too late to begin anew. Interest in one's partner serves as the catalyst for a profound connection between spouses, empowering them to cultivate a more fulfilling marital bond.

Modern times have seen a shift in gender roles, with women no longer solely responsible for homemaking duties. Yet, it's not uncommon to hear a woman confess that she lacks culinary or housekeeping skills. Astonishingly, the cleanliness of the home has even become a point of contention, leading to marital breakdown in some instances. Husbands may express frustration when the house isn't impeccably clean despite the fact that their wives do not work outside the home. Demonstrating interest in one's partner offers a simple solution to these issues. If a wife lacks culinary skills, her husband will undoubtedly appreciate her efforts to learn and prepare his favorite dishes. Each instance becomes a tangible sign of her investment in their relationship. The same principle applies to maintaining a clean home. A wife, in pursuit of her husband's happiness, will strive to maintain a tidy living space. If this proves challenging, she will explore alternatives, such as seeking help from cleaning services. In turn, the husband will seek ways to delight his wife by attending to her preferences, showcasing his dedication to her well-being.

Interest in one's partner often propels the development of new skills, as illustrated by the widespread adoption of modern technology. Over half the world's population is now connected via smartphones and social media. Remarkably, individuals in their 70s and beyond have embraced these digital tools to stay connected with loved ones. Although typing on a touchscreen without physical keys may be baffling to older generations, their determination to stay in touch with family and friends drives them to master these new technologies. The majority of today's generation effortlessly navigates smartphones and social media platforms, adapting to rapid technological advancements. This adaptability and willingness to embrace new skills are testaments to the power of interest in maintaining meaningful connections.

A brief anecdote highlights the stark contrast between those who embrace mutual support and those who neglect it. On one occasion, I found myself seated in a restaurant across from a couple, sharing neighboring tables for a duration of 90 minutes.

During this time, the woman was engrossed in taking selfies with her phone while adjusting her hair, while the man contentedly munched on chips and salsa while awaiting their meal. As time passed, the man's discomfort became evident, and instead of requesting more salsa, he retrieved his own phone and began watching sports. Meanwhile, the woman remained absorbed in her virtual world. Intrigued by this dynamic, I decided to extend my stay, ordering coffee and dessert after my dinner to observe their interactions further. When their meals arrived, the woman finally put down her phone, consumed only a fraction of her food, and resumed her selfie session. She signaled to her husband to request a takeout box for her meal. The husband, in a considerate gesture, finished his own meal, sampled some of his wife's dishes, and eventually requested the takeout box. They departed together, and if asked about their evening, they would likely report that they enjoyed a dinner outing as a couple. This scenario underscores the potential consequences of neglecting interest in one another. I am confident that many of us have encountered similar situations in our own lives.

The second crucial element for fostering mutual support is respect. Following the demonstration of genuine interest in each other's desires and dreams, respect forms the bedrock of support. Society often perpetuates gender stereotypes, attributing specific preferences and activities to men and women. For example, it is common to hear that men enjoy activities like hunting or fishing while women prefer shopping or leisurely walks in the park. Although many couples initially claim to share the same interests, the realities of married life frequently reveal differences in preferences and tastes. Respecting these differences is paramount. It implies that, at times, a wife may need to engage in fishing to accompany her husband, just as a husband may accompany his wife on shopping trips, even if he expects she won't make any purchases. Showing interest entails maintaining a positive attitude during these shared activities, patiently dedicating time, perhaps even two hours, and helping decide between two dresses, for instance. Conversely, showing disrespect might involve leaving to find a bar while one's partner makes their choice.

The enchantment of mutual support doesn't lie solely in tolerating each other's activities and preferences but in active participation, as illustrated in the examples mentioned earlier. Scientific research on couple dynamics reinforces the significance of mutual support by highlighting its role in generating positive emotions while reducing anxiety and insecurity. Couples who wholeheartedly embrace mutual support are better equipped to navigate conflicts and readily extend forgiveness. This support engenders a heightened sense of closeness, understanding, and love within the marriage.

In conclusion, mutual support is not merely a desirable trait in a successful marriage; it is the very backbone upon which enduring and fulfilling partnerships are built. By nurturing genuine interest, respect, and active involvement in each other's lives, couples lay the foundation for a resilient, loving, and lasting union that thrives in the face of life's myriad challenges and joys. Cultivating mutual support is the key to establishing a solid and meaningful relationship that stands the test of time.

EXPECTATIONS

There isn't a husband or wife who doesn't have expectations of their partner. We all anticipate certain things from the person we share our lives with. Marriage begins with two individuals, like a spark, gradually leading them into an interaction whose outcome is the marital project. Each person contributes their personal attributes to shape the marital system, many of which are developed within their families of origin. Scholars of marital matters have identified three common categories of expectations:

a. Expectations that each individual holds for their partner.

b. Expectations regarding the institution of marriage itself.

c. Expectations stemming from their families of origin.

Marital expectations can be defined as what each person anticipates receiving from their partner, or at the very least, what they hope to see in them during their married life. These encompass the realization of social and intellectual dreams, equality between spouses (especially for women), sexual satisfaction, financial security, and more. Another marital expectation revolves around societal recognition, which some cultures express through changes in names and titles such as "Mrs." or "Madame."

Marital expectations begin to form within the family of origin. Communication styles, child-rearing practices, emotional intimacy, and financial management are all learned in the home environment. In general, newlyweds expect their love to grow stronger with each passing day, for their partner to provide support, especially in challenging situations, and for both parties to respect the sanctity of their marriage. They anticipate fidelity, commitment, and the fulfillment of their marital obligations.

One fundamental expectation is that of marrying the ideal man or woman. It's essential to dispel any misconceptions here. Everyone enters into marriage with the belief that they are marrying their ideal partner. Otherwise, marriage would be nothing more than a tasteless joke or a perilous game. But where does this notion of the "ideal spouse" come from? It originates from two primary sources: personal life experiences and one's surroundings. There is an overwhelming list of qualities individuals expect to find in their partner, including trustworthiness, supportiveness, mutual love, respect, and understanding. At times, these ideals are influenced by media representations or romantic fantasies, leading individuals to seek partners who align with the images and ideals they hold in their minds. However, in practical terms, the ideal spouse is simply someone who balances material and non-material concerns while remaining firmly committed to their marital relationship.

It's crucial to note that society itself influences marital expectations, often presenting certain models of marital success and pressuring all couples to conform. The consequence of this pressure is that when a couple fails to meet societal expectations, they can experience frustration, leading to low marital satisfaction.

It's important to understand that there are differences in marital expectations between partners. Women often have a clearer idea of what they expect from their husbands, while men may be less certain. Women tend to be more in touch with their emotions and tend towards realism, whereas men may be more idealistic and sometimes evade or downplay relationship issues. However, after many years of marriage, women often show signs of disillusionment with their expectations, meaning they no longer harbor illusions about certain aspects of their relationship. This is where phrases like "I know him/her, they won't change... it's always the same..." often come into play.

Comparing marital expectations to the reality of the relationship can significantly impact marital satisfaction. Therefore, it's essential to align expectations with reality. Rather than basing expectations solely on the other person, each individual should orient their expectations towards themselves, focusing on what they can contribute to the marital relationship.

Navigating the intricate landscape of marital expectations is a complex journey that deeply influences the dynamics of a partnership. It's a terrain marked by a myriad of emotions, experiences, and external pressures. Let's delve deeper into some key aspects and considerations related to these expectations.

Unrealistic Expectations: The notion of an ideal partner is a common thread in discussions about marital expectations. Often, individuals enter marriage with sky-high ideals, assuming their spouse will effortlessly embody every quality they hold dear. Unrealistic expectations can set the stage for disappointment and dissatisfaction when the partner inevitably falls short of this unattainable standard. It's essential to recognize that no one is flawless, and everyone brings their own set of strengths and weaknesses into a marriage.

Societal Influences: Society plays a substantial role in shaping our expectations of marriage. Media, in particular, often portrays relationships in an idealized manner, emphasizing the romantic aspects while downplaying the practical challenges. These portrayals can lead individuals to believe that love alone is enough to sustain a marriage, overlooking the importance of communication, compromise, and shared responsibilities. Consequently, couples may find themselves unprepared for the real-world complexities of married life.

Adjusting Expectations: As couples journey through their married life, they inevitably encounter various realities that challenge their initial expectations. It's crucial for partners to engage in ongoing conversations about their evolving desires and needs. What may have been a priority at the outset of the relationship may shift over time. Adaptability and open communication are key to ensuring that both individuals continue to feel fulfilled within the marriage.

Balancing Personal Growth: Another aspect of expectations revolves around personal growth within the context of marriage. Couples often anticipate mutual support for their individual aspirations and ambitions. However, it's vital to strike a balance between individual growth and the growth of the partnership. Encouraging each other's pursuits while maintaining a strong connection is a delicate equilibrium that can lead to a fulfilling and harmonious marriage.

Conflict Resolution: Discrepancies between expectations and reality can give rise to conflicts within a marriage. How couples navigate these conflicts is instrumental in determining the overall satisfaction in the relationship. Effective conflict resolution strategies, such as active listening, empathy, and compromise, can help bridge the gap between what was anticipated and what has transpired.

Cultural Variations: Expectations in marriage can significantly differ across cultures. Different societies have distinct norms, traditions, and values that shape how couples approach their relationships. Recognizing and respecting these cultural nuances is essential for maintaining harmony in a multicultural marriage.

Embracing Imperfections: Ultimately, a key lesson in managing expectations in marriage is learning to embrace imperfections. No one is without their flaws, and relationships are not immune to challenges. However, it is precisely these imperfections and challenges that offer opportunities for growth, deeper understanding, and the development of resilience as a couple.

In conclusion, expectations in marriage are a deeply ingrained aspect of the journey, influenced by personal experiences, societal ideals, and cultural backgrounds. Acknowledging and managing these expectations with a sense of realism, adaptability, and open communication can pave the way for a more fulfilling and enduring partnership. Marriage, in its true essence, is a dynamic and evolving union that thrives when both individuals actively engage in nurturing and strengthening their connection, even as the landscape of their expectations shifts and transforms over time.

RESPONSIBILITIES IN MARRIAGE

Scholars of marital matters identify five major causes of marital conflicts, and among them is the distribution of household responsibilities. These conflicts have become more acute in recent times due to a lack of time. It's common for both partners to work outside the home, and when there are children, attending their school and extracurricular activities consumes time. For these and other reasons, now more than ever, couples must organize household chores in such a way that responsibilities are evenly distributed. Research shows that the effective allocation of household chores is as vital to marital satisfaction as fidelity and sexual intimacy. As I mentioned in the section on mutual support, being sensitive to ensuring that no one is burdened with all the household tasks is a sign of mutual support.

There are classic stereotypes that predefine certain roles based on gender. For instance, many people believe that women should be responsible for cooking while men should handle yard work. However, there are no laws that endorse these stereotypes. In many families, men enjoy cooking, and women don't mind getting their hands dirty in the garden. Of course, most prefer their partner's cooking, as women are generally better cooks, infusing their meals with the magical ingredient of love.

Both partners possess the necessary skills for household chores. The spirit of task distribution should adhere to the principles of teamwork. Unfortunately, women are often burdened with a heavy load, even when they work outside the home. After dedicating 40 or more hours to a full-time job, they are still expected to perform full-time duties as homemakers, wives, and mothers, with all the tasks and responsibilities this entails. The pace of modern society's life doesn't always allow for stable family schedules as it once did. Synchronizing family calendars between work, school, and home would enable having a hot meal on the table at a certain time when the whole family is gathered to eat. However, this is no longer easy, but that doesn't mean couples should give up their efforts to distribute responsibilities in a way that preserves these sacred moments of family togetherness.

The distribution of chores should be based on the principle of equality. Men and women are equal in dignity by virtue of their creation and share the same responsibility for running the household. Gender differences are a wealth that brings different yet equally valuable skills to enhance interaction and coexistence within the family. It's important to remind each other that the goal is the same for both, and therefore, teamwork remains of paramount importance. Even though each has different responsibilities, the plan is the same. Therefore, it doesn't matter who takes out the trash or bathes the children. What matters is that both agree on the distribution of responsibilities. And this doesn't always mean that the tasks will turn out exactly the same for both.

The best results are achieved through effective communication. Many studies indicate that communication that includes details of when, where, and how tasks should be done prevents confusion and promotes better use of time, energy, talent, and money. When spouses maintain good communication about household chores, anxiety levels are low, and there is greater satisfaction in the relationship. Whenever possible, it's better for the distribution to be somewhat fixed, with some flexibility in case of necessary changes. When negotiating responsibilities is a daily occurrence, there is a greater likelihood of arguments, wasted time, and conflict.

Business techniques for distributing responsibilities can be useful at home. Companies allocate tasks based on the talents and interests of each employee, maximizing performance and productivity. The combination of talents and interests leads to higher job satisfaction and ensures stability. Similarly, within the household, spouses can divide chores based on their talents and interests. The result is always better when someone can fulfill their responsibilities not only because they have a talent for it but also because they enjoy doing it. Therefore, it's more effective to distribute chores based on talent rather than gender.

In the practical implementation of distribution, some basic rules should be followed. The first is to create a list of all the chores that need attention. This list is not arbitrary; it must indicate the priority and urgency of each task. For example, painting the house is not as urgent as cleaning the bathrooms. Prioritizing tasks requires negotiation between spouses. It's common for what is important and urgent for one may not be the same for the other. There are some tasks that no one enjoys but also don't require special skills, such as, ironically, cleaning the bathrooms. For these tasks, it's more advisable to take turns so that one person doesn't end up as the bathroom cleaner for the next 16 years until they pass the torch to the eldest daughter.

The assignment of responsibilities can also vary under special circumstances. For instance, if the wife, in addition to working, starts studying, the husband can take over bathing the children, helping with their homework, and preparing dinner, even if this was previously the wife's task. The allocation of tasks should be realistic, as I've already mentioned. But there are cases where someone takes on responsibility for which they don't have much talent. In these situations, the spouse should offer positive feedback, not criticism. If the husband is in charge of making the bed in the morning and consistently leaves the sheets misaligned, the wife would do well not to ridicule him, criticize him, or disrespect him. Instead, she should support and help him improve in performing this task. It's true that some husbands are better cooks than their wives. However, the man shouldn't throw it in her face during an argument and certainly shouldn't tell her she's "good for nothing." A quick aside, if I may. It's true that controlling what one says when they're upset requires effort. But to say to your partner that they're "good for nothing"? With this statement, and by putting down your partner, you're confessing to being a loser as well. Remember: the team wins, or the team loses. Speaking to your partner in such a derogatory and hurtful manner is very offensive. Unless a marriage has been arranged by others, if one spouse is good for nothing, then the other who chose them for marriage must also be good for nothing.

It may not seem like a big deal, but it's very important to appreciate your partner's effort in fulfilling their responsibilities at home. You should "cheer them on," as it's commonly said. I have the privilege of sharing dinner with friends several times a month. It's a custom in their family to thank the wife for cooking. It starts with the husband, followed by the children, and I don't lag behind. I really appreciate these gestures. The wife always responds with a reward. Her reaction is to ask what we want to eat the next day or offer a delicious dessert. This means she enjoys cooking for her family. Along with the detail of appreciating your partner's effort, there's another powerful gesture you can make for your partner: give them a break. Offering to take on your partner's tasks is a demonstration of love, mutual support, and affection. These gestures go straight to your partner's heart and earn points for the team.

Certain researchers have studied various methods of collaboration in household chores, focusing on tasks that couples perform together, such as cooking. These experts formulated four categories, all equally valuable. The first category is silent collaboration, where each person performs their tasks without much conversation. The second category is that of an expert and an assistant. In this style of collaboration, one spouse takes the lead and gets help from the other. The third category is coordinated collaboration. The couple verbally coordinates their collaboration during execution. The last category is separate collaboration. In this case, each member of the couple performs their tasks in a different physical space.

Regardless of the couple's collaboration style, the equitable distribution of responsibilities at home is undoubtedly a key ingredient for marital satisfaction. Ultimately, there is no one-size-fits-all formula. What's important is that the couple continues to work as a team. There's no need to document performance data for chores. Instead, commit to doing what contributes to the family's well-being and the well-being of each spouse. As the family experiences different phases, it's expected that the distribution of responsibilities and chores will change.

In the ever-evolving landscape of marriage and family life, the importance of effectively balancing responsibilities within the household cannot be overstated. As society undergoes changes, such as both partners working outside the home and the complexities of managing children's schedules, the need for equitable distribution of tasks becomes more pressing. Researchers and experts have identified this as a critical factor in maintaining marital satisfaction, often on par with fidelity and sexual intimacy.

Traditionally, rigid gender stereotypes have prescribed specific roles within the family unit. Women were expected to take on the bulk of household chores, while men handled tasks seen as more 'masculine,' such as yard work. However, contemporary families challenge these norms as both partners bring diverse skills and interests to the table. Today, we recognize that abilities and passions are not confined by gender, and a husband may excel in the kitchen just as much as his wife. It's the uniqueness of each partner's contributions that enriches the family's daily life.

In the face of hectic modern schedules, maintaining a sense of togetherness can be challenging, but it remains essential. The rhythm of contemporary life doesn't always allow for the structured family meals that were once the norm. Yet, couples should strive to preserve these sacred moments of family bonding, even if it means adapting to a new schedule.

Equality should serve as the cornerstone of responsibility allocation in a marriage. Men and women share equal dignity by virtue of their creation, and the responsibility of running a household falls on both partners. Although their roles may differ, their ultimate objective is the same, emphasizing the importance of teamwork. It's not about who takes out the trash or bathes the children; it's about mutual agreement and collaboration in the distribution of responsibilities.

Effective communication plays a pivotal role in ensuring that these responsibilities are distributed fairly. By discussing the specifics of when, where, and how tasks should be completed, couples can minimize confusion and optimize the use of their time, energy, talents, and financial resources. This open dialogue not only prevents misunderstandings but also contributes to a deeper sense of satisfaction in the relationship.

While the distribution of responsibilities should ideally remain somewhat consistent, flexibility is key. Life can throw curveballs, and couples must adapt to changing circumstances. Daily negotiations over responsibilities can lead to unnecessary tension and conflicts, so finding a routine that accommodates both partners' needs and schedules is essential.

Taking inspiration from business strategies, couples can optimize their task distribution. Just as companies assign tasks based on employees' talents and interests to maximize productivity and job satisfaction, couples can benefit from aligning household chores with their strengths and passions.

This approach ensures that each partner is motivated to complete their tasks to the best of their abilities.

Practicality should guide the allocation of responsibilities, with a focus on prioritizing tasks based on urgency and importance. Some chores may be universally disliked but require no special skills. In such cases, taking turns can be a fair solution, preventing one partner from being saddled with a particularly undesirable task for an extended period.

In times of special circumstances, such as one partner taking on additional responsibilities like studying while working, the roles may need to be adjusted temporarily. The key is flexibility and understanding, with partners supporting each other rather than criticizing shortcomings. Encouraging each other's efforts and offering assistance where needed can strengthen the partnership.

Acknowledging and appreciating each other's efforts is paramount. Expressing gratitude for a partner's contributions fosters a positive atmosphere within the relationship. Small gestures like thanking your partner for cooking or lending a helping hand can go a long way in reinforcing mutual respect and love.

Researchers have explored various methods of collaborating on household tasks, whether through silent cooperation, one leading as an expert while the other assists, coordinating efforts verbally, or working separately in different spaces. Regardless of the chosen approach, the underlying principle remains the same: equitable distribution of responsibilities is vital for marital satisfaction.

In conclusion, as couples navigate the intricacies of modern life, the equitable distribution of responsibilities within the household remains a cornerstone of marital success. While there is no one-size-fits-all solution, fostering open communication, embracing flexibility, and appreciating each other's contributions can lead to a harmonious and fulfilling partnership. Just as the family unit evolves, so too should the approach to sharing responsibilities, ensuring that love and understanding continue to thrive at the heart of every marriage.

THE EDUCATION OF CHILDREN

In my book published in January 2016, "I Can't Stand You Anymore! How to Guide a Teenager," I argue that educating children is the noblest task of parents. It is the source that gives them life, although this same task also consumes a lot of energy. The family is a sacred space and a place of celebration where parents have the responsibility to create a healthy environment that promotes the development of everyone, including themselves. In every family, there are the best parents and the best children. The couple's task is to ensure that constant adjustment to changes safeguards harmony and the bonds of love and affection that keep the family together. What is the current context of children's education? Why does this context present an opportunity for a good marital experience?

The social context in which children are growing up today is unique in human history. No one can ignore the rapid social changes that parents must adapt to in the education of their children. Couples are faced with phenomena such as technological advances and their toys. The internet, cell phones, social media, and video games have created parallel spaces and serious competition in the education of children. These spaces saturate children with information that, in many cases, parents are not familiar with. In past times, for example, parents were respected for their life experience, wisdom, and greater knowledge than their children. Nowadays, all of this is relative. As long as Google and the virtual community exist, parents must be careful not to provide incorrect information to their children. Even at the age of 4, a child is capable of contradicting their parents based on research they conducted on the internet. I had the opportunity to talk to a nine-year-old who told me that because of his fear of storms, he had become an "expert" in meteorology and had a lot of information related to weather phenomena. The classic responses of parents no longer hold. Saying "it's nothing" is not enough when the child knows that a lightning strike can kill them.

Another element of the current context in which children are growing up has to do with all the external influences they are exposed to. The media bombard their minds from a very young age with information about beauty, power, money, success, and fame. The incidence of eating disorders such as anorexia nervosa is increasing among the child population. This situation, which creates a lot of insecurity in parents, adds to the easy and premature access that children have to alcohol, drugs, and irresponsible sex. Social sciences show that young people today easily engage in high-risk behaviors. All this flood of information that children receive daily leaves spouses in a vulnerable position because the information from their own upbringing is no longer very useful to them. Some time ago, a video circulated on the internet showing a 9-year-old calling the police because his mother had given him three spankings with a belt, based on a report from the school. The child explained to the police that he had rights and that his mother could not and should not punish him. Upon seeing the police, the woman panicked and asked the officer if she would go to jail. The mother and the child were surprised by the policeman's response because he told the child that he would apply the same punishment if he were his father. We know that this is not the typical way to resolve these issues. In fact, children can intimidate their parents when they talk about their rights not to be punished.

What is the effect of raising children on the quality of marriage? The context I mentioned above demonstrates that raising children has become a very delicate task, surrounded by many challenges. Faced with parents' powerlessness in the face of modern social changes, raising children offers the couple a great opportunity to work as a team. Social sciences have shown that during the years of child-rearing, all the effort and attention of spouses are focused on them. Some scholars interpret this focus on children as a weakness of marriage. However, reality presents a different picture. Spouses have to collaborate closely on the project of raising their children. This begins with establishing a philosophy of education. This understanding of education is informed by the values of the spouses. Spirituality in the life of a couple also has an impact on children. I knew of a young couple who did not practice any religion. When their first child was born, the couple decided to go to church every Sunday with their baby to introduce this weekly structure that includes a space for spiritual life from an early age. The young couple commented that they didn't care much about the religious confession their child would choose when he became an adult because they only wanted to ensure they instilled this habit.

One sign of success for the couple as a team is the organization of their children's education. I'm not saying that the success or failure of children in their lives is the responsibility of parents. Since raising children is more complex today than before, as I explained above, the collaboration of spouses to achieve a good result is a very important ingredient for marital satisfaction. Just as children have access to a lot of information on a wide range of topics, couples also have the ability to consult all available material for raising their children. Science has helped establish parameters that can guide parents in this beautiful and delicate task. There is a lot of literature on education that helps couples understand how to support each stage of their children's development.

As an illustration of what I just mentioned above, I would like to address an aspect of children's education that represents a great opportunity for a fulfilling marriage. This is the benefit of family meals for family members. Various recent studies have examined the impact of family meals on the functioning and behaviors of family members. Eating together as a family is an opportunity to be together and interact as a family unit. Some of the benefits of these moments are the health and well-being of children and adolescents. Family meals involve interacting in meal preparation, assigning roles, and communicating. Family meals are beneficial for socialization and a child's development. The dining table is the privileged place to model good attitudes and shape children. It is a team effort for the couple. These types of events are the platform for socializing, having fun, recreation, and cultural learning. Nowadays, it is common for family members to be separated during the day. Children go to school, and parents go to work. In lower and middle-class families, both parents work long hours. In many cases, eating together is the only activity the family can do regularly. Experience has shown that frequent family meals do not happen automatically. These moments have to be intentionally scheduled, prepared, and carried out by each family.

Another benefit of family meals is enjoying and educating about healthy eating. It is an opportunity for parents to be good role models, showing their children that the quality of food has an impact on health. If parents make an effort to include vegetables and natural juices in family meals, children will assimilate these good habits from an early age. Therefore, spouses must be aware of the scope of their responsibility in making decisions regarding family nutrition and the implications of these decisions on their own health and that of their children. Recent scientific research has shown a correlation between the frequency of family meals and increased consumption of fruits, vegetables, grains, and calcium-rich foods. The family environment offers an excellent opportunity for children to eat healthily.

Eating together as a family and conversing around the table provides an excellent opportunity for children and adolescents to learn new vocabulary through stories, cultural knowledge, beliefs, customs, traditions, etc. In turn, children and young people share their life experiences outside the home at the table. It has been proven that conversations during family meals have a very positive impact on reading and vocabulary in preschoolers and older children. Seven or more family meals per week result in better school grades.

The simplest and most effective way to get involved in the lives of adolescent children is to establish family meals. Young people who share more meals with their parents are less likely to smoke, drink alcohol, or use drugs. Stress and depression levels in teenagers are significantly reduced with frequent family meals. The maximum benefit is achieved when both parents are present. A good number of studies indicate that frequent family meals help reduce the incidence of high-risk behaviors in adolescents, such as promiscuity, low self-esteem, school problems, and eating disorders.

Family meals go beyond just nourishing the body; they nourish the soul and strengthen familial bonds. The act of coming together around the dinner table offers a precious opportunity for family members to connect on a deeper level. It's a time when everyone can put aside their busy schedules, gadgets, and distractions to engage in meaningful conversations. During these moments, parents have a chance to listen to their children's thoughts, concerns, and aspirations, fostering open communication and trust.

Moreover, family meals provide a platform for parents to instill important values and life lessons in their children. As parents share stories, traditions, and cultural knowledge, they are passing down their family's heritage and values. These gatherings become a living history lesson, teaching children about their roots and the world around them. Parents can also use this time to discuss topics such as respect, empathy, kindness, and responsibility, guiding their children towards becoming well-rounded individuals.

The benefits of regular family meals extend to academic success as well. When children engage in conversations with their parents and siblings during mealtimes, they are exposed to a broader vocabulary and a more extensive range of ideas. This exposure can significantly improve their language skills, critical thinking abilities, and overall academic performance. Studies have shown that children who participate in frequent family meals tend to excel in school and have better problem-solving skills.

In addition to the educational and emotional advantages, family meals are an opportunity to introduce children to diverse cuisines and encourage them to develop healthy eating habits. When parents model good dietary choices by including a variety of fruits, vegetables, lean proteins, and whole grains on the dinner table, children are more likely to adopt these habits. This can have a long-lasting impact on their overall health and well-being, reducing the risk of obesity, chronic diseases, and unhealthy eating behaviors.

Furthermore, family meals are a time for children to learn about food preparation and teamwork. Involving children in meal preparation, even in small ways like setting the table or helping with simple cooking tasks, not only teaches them practical life skills but also fosters a sense of responsibility and contribution to the family unit. It's a way of demonstrating that everyone in the family plays a vital role in its functioning.

From the perspective of maintaining a strong and healthy marriage, family meals offer couples a chance to reconnect and share the responsibilities of child-rearing. It's a shared commitment to providing a nurturing and supportive environment for their children. Collaborating on meal planning, preparation, and cleanup can promote a sense of unity and cooperation between spouses. It also allows couples to step away from their individual roles and work together as a team towards a common goal, strengthening their partnership.

In conclusion, family meals hold a unique and invaluable place in the lives of both children and couples. They provide an opportunity for bonding, communication, and education while promoting healthy eating habits and academic success. Through the simple act of sharing a meal, families can create lasting memories and nurture the relationships that are at the core of a thriving and fulfilling life. So, let's not underestimate the power of gathering around the dinner table and cherishing these moments with our loved ones.

LEISURE TIME

The use of leisure time can also be defined as recreational time. People get married to be happy. The ability of the couple to enjoy their leisure time is an essential ingredient for a happy and lasting marriage. Where there is no fun, boredom, and anxiety dominate the atmosphere. When this becomes the norm, divorce is on the horizon. The use of leisure time or recreation is experienced in various areas. Here, I mention four. The first is for each individual to do what they enjoy. The second is having fun together as spouses. The third is having fun with children, and the fourth is having fun with friends. All four forms should be used if there are children in the family.

Regarding this section, a crucial step is to properly allocate leisure time. Taking into account the different categories mentioned, recreation should be included in the overall time management. Important studies indicate that when there is an imbalance in how and when the couple has fun, there is a higher incidence of anxiety, boredom, and fatigue. Work, children, and other social commitments don't leave much free time during the day. Having leisure time and planning recreational activities as a couple is also not easy. This requires a conscious effort from both parties.

Each member of the couple should maintain their own healthy personal pastimes. It is the responsibility

87

of the other to support them without resorting to control. One of the mistakes couples make early in the relationship is that due to one person's insecurity, the other is forced to completely forget their life before marriage. I have known cases where one of them has to destroy their old photos to avoid provoking jealousy from the partner. It is also not acceptable to ask your partner to end their friendship from when they were single. As I mentioned in the chapter on friendships, the world is vast, and the interaction between two people cannot fill it. The personal recreations of the members of the couple are generally done with friends who share the same interests. It's worth repeating that each person should have their own time to have fun.

Let's talk a bit about having fun as a couple. During the dating phase, preferences for ways to have fun together start to emerge. This time is ideal for refining and aligning your tastes. Even after marriage and when you have children, it is important for spouses to plan alone time to do something they both enjoy. It's sad to hear someone complain about not having any common fun activities with their partner. One of the classic complaints relates to music and going out at night. This is not a gender problem. Sometimes, it's the woman who enjoys dancing and going out, while the man prefers to stay at home. In other cases, it's the opposite. In any case, it is crucial for the well-being of the couple that spouses find common recreational interests. In theory, this should not be difficult since these affinities should have been known before marrying someone. When there are no common interests in recreation, the first entertaining task is to find them. If there is nothing they both enjoy, then one will accompany the other in their pastimes, willingly and with a good attitude. Just as a wife can enjoy her husband's soccer game (even if she doesn't understand the rules), the husband can spend two hours with his wife at the stores (even if she can't decide on anything). Having fun as a couple alone is an ingredient for connection, communication, and intimacy.

The third category of fun is with children. Schedules are very diverse and demanding. School-aged children are just as busy as their parents. Everyone is racing against the clock. Regardless of available financial means, spouses must organize moments of fun as a family. These events strengthen the bonds between children and their parents. The benefits for the well-being of children are invaluable, with the most important being that children feel loved by their parents. This greatly enhances their self-esteem. If someone is not willing to love their children and dedicate time to them, they may need to reconsider having children. This reminds me of Franco de Vita's song (No Basta). No one can buy their children's happiness with money or material things. Children need the love of their parents, with or without the trendy toys they can buy. In some cases, these family fun experiences can include cousins and close friends of the children, exposing them to the experience of sharing, interacting, and socializing with other children.

The fourth category of fun is with other families. Typically, couples socialize with other couples of similar ages. Friendship with them forms a support network in which different couples share their experiences. When there are arguments within the marriage, it is common to turn to these friendships for advice, thanks to the trust that has developed during shared recreational activities. But it's worth noting here that having fun with other couples should not be a way to mask difficulties within the marriage. It has been observed that some couples who have problems resort to socializing with other couples to avoid direct interaction with each other. When this is the case, there is a tendency to integrate with other people and thus avoid the partner. In some circles, socializing with other married couples means that women get together separately, and men do the same. This type of activity does not fall into the category of fun with couples.

Creating spaces for leisure and fun is a good ingredient for a fulfilling marriage. In the play, humans express themselves freely and release their stress. Having fun is healthy for individuals, couples, and families. Continuously organizing and planning time for these moments is a sign that the couple wants to continue strengthening their relationship.

Leisure time plays a crucial role in nurturing a happy and thriving marriage, as well as fostering personal growth and well-being. As we delve deeper into the various aspects of leisure and recreation within a marital context, it becomes evident that it is not just a luxury but a necessity for the health of the relationship.

The first aspect we discussed is the importance of each individual pursuing their own interests and hobbies. In a healthy marriage, partners should encourage and support each other in these endeavors. It's essential to understand that maintaining one's individuality and passion is not a threat to the relationship but a way to enrich it. When both partners have the freedom to explore their own interests, they bring more to the table in terms of personal growth and fulfillment, which ultimately benefits the partnership as a whole.

Another critical dimension of leisure time in marriage is spending quality time together as a couple. While it's true that each person should have their own interests, finding common activities that both partners enjoy is a bonding experience. Whether it's a shared hobby, a regular date night, or simply relaxing together at home, these moments strengthen the emotional connection between spouses. It's also an opportunity to escape from the stresses of daily life and focus on nurturing the relationship itself.

Moreover, when children enter the picture, managing leisure time can become even more challenging. Juggling work, school schedules, extracurricular activities, and family commitments can be overwhelming. However, it is precisely during these times that carving out moments for family fun becomes paramount. Engaging in activities that all family members can enjoy not only creates lasting memories but also reinforces the bonds between parents and children. These shared experiences provide children with a sense of security, belonging, and love, which are vital for their emotional development.

Furthermore, fostering friendships with other couples is an essential aspect of a well-rounded married life. Socializing with other families allows for a broader support network and an opportunity to exchange insights and advice. However, it's important to strike a balance. While it's healthy to spend time with friends, it should not serve as a distraction from addressing any issues within the marriage. Open and honest communication within the marital relationship should always take precedence.

In summary, leisure time and recreation are not just about having fun; they are about building and maintaining a strong and fulfilling marriage. It's about creating a space where individuality is celebrated, shared experiences are cherished, and family bonds are strengthened. Recognizing the significance of leisure within a marriage and actively working to incorporate it into your life can lead to a more joyful, resilient, and enduring partnership. So, as you navigate the complexities of married life, remember the importance of laughter, shared adventures, and the simple pleasure of spending quality time with the one you love.

HABITS

Human beings are generally understood as creatures of habit. Each person develops their own way of doing things. Habits range from the way of thinking and reacting to the way of dressing and arranging the house. It is common to hear from couples that part of the attraction to the other person is because they like their habits. Here, it is important to be honest and sincere. For example, a person with a low tolerance for smoke will not feel attracted to someone who smokes regularly. Life as a couple is a very close daily coexistence. Each one has to live and coexist with the habits of the other. Successfully managing each other's habits is an ingredient that adds a lot of flavors to the marital relationship. Let's delve a bit into habits, which I will present in five categories based on each partner's personality.

The first category of habits arises from each person's organizational style. When both coincide in their particular style, getting used to each other is not very difficult. For example, if both like things very clean, orderly, and in their place, you can expect the TV remote controls to always be in the same place, the bed to be clean and tidy every day, and the bread, eggs, milk, fruits, and vegetables to always be properly stored in the refrigerator. In some cases, dirty laundry might even be neatly folded in the hamper. Two people with this style function optimally when everything is always in its place. In family living activities, these couples generally eat the same thing every Monday, watch the same TV show at set times, go to the same restaurant every Sunday, and buy the same household items at the same store. Organized people find security and pleasure in routine and react negatively to unforeseen changes. The conscious effort to adapt is more challenging when the partners have different organizational styles. If one is very organized and the other doesn't care about the messy closet, which looks like a battlefield, it becomes necessary to find ways to adapt so that neither feels pressured to adopt the other person's style systemically.

Another important aspect of habits is sociability. There are many ways to express social habits, often understood by the number of friends one has and how frequently one goes to parties. Based on this, a person can be considered introverted or reserved, extroverted or outgoing. The habits of the couple determine their communication style and how they resolve conflicts. A very sociable person is generally more willing to express their feelings or opinions on any matter. They are not afraid to address issues that require it, even when there are differences of opinion. They may also be more explosive but do not hold grudges. On the other hand, more reserved or introverted people avoid confrontations and keep things to themselves. They dislike arguing and may make unexpected decisions. It is likely that an introverted couple may have a quieter interaction but may be harboring genuine "time bombs." On the other hand, two extroverted people may maintain a lively atmosphere at home without holding grudges.

Another determining factor of habits is the desire to please. Couples use the word "thoughtful" to refer to the person who is sensitive to the other's preferences and seeks ways to please them. Being well taken care of is certainly enjoyable. And when both partners have this sensitivity, pleasing each other with thoughtful gestures is common. Conversely, some couples struggle to use thoughtful gestures to please each other. The challenge lies in the differences in habits. Sometimes, these differences are interpreted as manipulation or lack of interest. In the midst of a conflict, the person trying to please their partner may be accused of being manipulative. And, of course, the indifferent person receives the free diagnosis of lacking love.

Openness to change is another essential factor to consider when discussing habits and customs. Every couple establishes their routines, rituals, and traditions. Harmony in married life largely depends on how routines are managed. As mentioned earlier, human beings are creatures of habit, so it is expected that changes are not always welcome. I can say with certainty that the only person who always wants change is a baby with a wet diaper. The rest of the population prefers to live in their routines. Changes in married life or in daily activities require clear agreements, especially when each person reacts to change differently. Those who prefer to stay in the same routine see change as a threat to stability. On the opposite end, those who are more open to change may find the same routines boring.

Emotional stability is another element that determines a person's habits. In general, every human being functions better in stable conditions. Emotional stability ensures a certain degree of predictability. The first step to achieving stability is self-acceptance. Experts in self-esteem issues claim that each person must accept themselves as they indeed are, including their qualities and their limitations or flaws. This self-acceptance is expressed in daily life. Personal insecurity leads to emotional instability. The social system generates mechanisms that promote instability to sell us certain products. For example, women without actual weight issues sometimes feel fat wearing a size zero. When this is their mindset, any comment or suggestion in that regard from their spouse, no matter how innocent, can easily lead to a big problem. When we lack emotional stability, we may commit certain injustices. The most common one is blaming others for our emotional states. When someone unjustly externalizes that their partner's treatment is the cause of their unhappiness or bad mood, they are absolving themselves of the personal responsibility to control their feelings.

In conclusion, habits, as an essential ingredient in a relationship, go hand in hand with accepting the chosen travel companion from the dating stage. To achieve this, one must "bury and forget" the personal project of changing the other person. Many individuals become disillusioned when they see that their partner doesn't change. In situations where the problem is related to the other person's habits, the fundamental question is, when did these habits appear? In many cases, the honest answer is that the person has always been this way. The second question is, why don't you like a habit you've known about all along? The honest answer is, "I never really liked that." The third question is, "then why did you marry him/her?" The typical answer is, "because I thought they would change." I believe this approach is unfair because it imposes the responsibility for change on someone who may not be aware of it or committed to it.

Understanding and managing habits is a crucial aspect of any successful relationship. It not only involves recognizing each other's habits but also finding ways to coexist harmoniously while respecting each other's individuality. Let's delve deeper into the complexities of these five categories of habits and explore some strategies for navigating them within a partnership.

Organizational Styles: When it comes to habits rooted in organization, open communication is key. Partners with similar organizational styles may find it easier to adapt to each other's routines, but those with different approaches can still make it work. It might involve compromise, like designating specific areas for one partner to be organized while allowing the other more flexibility in other spaces. The key is to appreciate each other's strengths and find common ground.

Sociability: Understanding the sociability habits of your partner can help improve communication. Couples with contrasting sociability levels can learn from each other. Extroverted partners can encourage their introverted counterparts to express themselves more openly, while introverted partners can provide stability and reflection during conflicts. The key is to create a safe and non-judgmental space for both personality types to thrive.

Desire to Please: Thoughtfulness and attentiveness to each other's needs can significantly strengthen a relationship. Partners who struggle with this aspect should engage in open conversations about their preferences and ways they'd like to be shown love and care. It's important to realize that thoughtful gestures may manifest differently in each person, and recognizing and appreciating these differences is vital.

Openness to Change: Coping with change is a challenge for most people. In a relationship, understanding each other's comfort zones and willingness to adapt to change can lead to healthier discussions and decision-making. For example, setting clear expectations about changes in routines or life events can reduce anxiety and provide a sense of control. Partners can also plan occasional changes together to keep the relationship exciting while respecting each other's need for stability.

Emotional Stability: Building emotional stability is an ongoing process that requires self-awareness and self-acceptance. Partners should encourage each other to work on their emotional well-being, possibly through therapy or self-help resources. It's crucial to remember that one person cannot solely be responsible for another's emotional state. Instead, both partners should support each other's emotional growth and help create a stable and nurturing environment in the relationship.

In addition to understanding and navigating these habits, couples need to maintain open lines of communication. Regular check-ins and discussions about individual and shared goals, values, and expectations can help strengthen the foundation of any relationship. Remember that no two individuals are exactly alike, and differences in habits can be a source of growth and enrichment rather than conflict.

Furthermore, it's important to be patient and compassionate with each other as you work through your habits. Change often takes time, and it's unrealistic to expect immediate transformations. What's more important is the willingness to grow and evolve together, even when faced with challenging habits or differences in personality.

Ultimately, a successful partnership is built on a foundation of acceptance, empathy, and a genuine desire to create a fulfilling and harmonious life together. Embracing each other's habits and differences can lead to a stronger, more resilient, and more loving relationship that stands the test of time.

FRIENDSHIPS

Friendship is understood as an emotional relationship between two individuals. It is the most common type of relationship among human beings. Marriage is formed by two friends. Friendship is an important stage at the beginning of a relationship, which enriches over time, eventually becoming a marital project. It is common to hear spouses say with great satisfaction, "I am marrying my best friend." Friendship entails a deep connection and lifelong loyalty. In this segment, we will consider the theme of friendship as a component of a fulfilling marriage, referring to friendships outside of the couple. To do this, I will divide my friends into two major groups. The first group consists of the individual friends of each spouse. The second group includes friends that both partners have in common.

The existence of both groups of friends is important in the life of the couple. These friendships should be nurtured with the flexibility and freedom that come with being friends. It's sad and, at the same time, a warning sign when a young suitor with no life experience asks their partner to stop having friends. Even sadder is when the girl accepts and respects such foolishness. It's like choosing sadness. And what is sadder than sadness itself? It's very regrettable that this same behavior happens among spouses. When someone tells me in counseling that they have no friends because their partner prohibited it, I know, with very little margin for error, who caused the problem. Obviously, it wasn't the person who prohibited friendships but the one who accepted such a prohibition. Friendship is a positive thing in a human's life. It's up to each individual to discern which of their friends is a bad influence and distance themselves from them. Before getting married, spouses have friends of both genders. Marriage is not a decree that ends friendships. True love is enjoyed with freedom. Someone who loves you allows you to have friends. Someone who forbids them doesn't love you and never will.

Each member of the couple is free to maintain their friendships from before marriage. In case these friendships represent a conflict of interest, it means they weren't true friendships. Friendship enriches life and is part of a crucial support network, especially when facing life's challenges. In addition to the friendship between spouses, it's healthy and positive for the marital relationship for each individual to have their own friends. It's common for circles of friends to have some "rituals," such as gathering to watch a game and have a beer; female friends may meet for shopping, beauty salon visits, or a meal. When geographical circumstances permit, it's favorable not to abandon these activities.

Prohibiting your partner from having healthy and open friendships leads to unnecessary arguments boredom, and opens the door to secret activities, which can lead to infidelity. Over the years, I have observed this sequence of events in marriages. The romantic relationship, its dynamics, and the feelings that accompany it do not compete with or confuse with the affection of friendship. There are seemingly hypocritical and senseless beliefs. Before marriage, a person has friendships with both men and women. After marriage, it is sometimes heard that a married man cannot have female friends, and a married woman cannot have male friends. These ideas reduce human beings to sexual robots. Friendship has nothing to do with gender. It's a connection that goes far beyond the physical and erotic aspects. Healthy relationships last forever. Friendships are spaces where one can vent and sometimes find good advice. When spouses isolate themselves from the world and selfishly try to create a bubble just for themselves, their relationship is at risk of suffocation and death due to lack of oxygen.

The other category of friendships is those within the couple. There is not as much of a problem in managing these friendships since both have access to them. The key is openness and honesty. Humans always seek another human to find the meaning of their life. Friendship is the only guarantee of peace and harmony in society. I have observed many groups of friendly couples who organize very uplifting activities for everyone. They travel together, pray together, support each other, and much more. This kind of interaction is a good ingredient for marital satisfaction. Certainly, the couple must exercise their good judgment in choosing their friends. Those who gather to get drunk or use drugs may also be good friends, but the activities they choose are destructive from any perspective and end up negatively affecting the marriage.

Building and nurturing friendships is a fundamental aspect of human existence. These bonds are not just about sharing a few laughs or passing the time; they are the threads that weave the intricate tapestry of our lives. They provide us with emotional support, a sense of belonging, and a safe space to express ourselves. Just as the saying goes, "A friend in need is a friend indeed."

In the context of marriage, friendships take on an even more significant role. They serve as the pillars upon which a strong and healthy relationship can thrive. When partners encourage each other to maintain their friendships, they are essentially nurturing the roots of their love tree. A robust support system outside the marriage can provide invaluable perspectives and help in times of need.

Furthermore, friendships can be a source of joy and excitement within a marriage. Imagine the joy of sharing stories about your friends' adventures or the anticipation of introducing your partner to new friends with shared interests. These experiences can rekindle the flames of passion and add a refreshing dimension to your relationship.

It's important to recognize that maintaining separate friendships does not diminish the bond between partners; instead, it enhances it. The ability to trust each other and allow for independence in social interactions is a testament to the strength of a relationship. In fact, it often leads to couples appreciating the uniqueness of their partner even more.

However, like any aspect of a relationship, balance is key. While it's essential to maintain individual friendships, it's equally important to prioritize quality time with your spouse. Communication and understanding each other's needs are essential to strike this balance successfully.

In today's interconnected world, the dynamics of friendships have evolved. The advent of social media and online communities has expanded our opportunities to make friends from all corners of the globe. While these digital connections can be valuable, it's essential not to neglect the importance of in-person friendships and face-to-face interactions, especially with your partner.

In conclusion, friendship is a precious asset in life, and it should be embraced and celebrated within the context of marriage. Encouraging each other to maintain friendships, both individual and mutual, can enrich your lives and strengthen your bond as a couple. Remember, true love is not possessive; it thrives on trust, openness, and the freedom to nurture friendships that bring joy, support, and meaning to your journey together. So, cherish your friends, and let your marriage flourish as a result.

GENDER

A well-known text from the Bible defines the peculiarities of each gender within the dynamics of marriage. In the book of Ephesians (5:22-33), Saint Paul instructs husbands on the appropriate attitudes in their interactions with their wives. The text can be summarized as follows: Women, respect your husbands. Husbands love your wives. Dr. Emerson Eggerichs has written a book about love and respect, in which, drawing inspiration from this biblical text, he demonstrates that women naturally desire to be loved, and men need to feel respected.

It is common for gender differences to be perceived as problematic. Harmony exists when things are properly aligned and everyone shares the same understanding and way of thinking. The religious order in which I spent my early missionary years had the motto: "One heart, one soul." When someone wants to express that things are going well in their marriage, it's common to hear something like this: "My partner and I are very happy. We think alike and have the same interests." However, for gender differences to be a favorable ingredient for marital satisfaction, both the man and the woman must retain their own essence. When this happens, differences become a source of richness rather than a problem. Women "read" through the lens of feeling loved or not. In everyday interactions, men should always keep this in mind and act accordingly. We all likely have many stories to share on this topic.

In a television commercial, we see a woman trying on several dresses to go out with her husband to buy ice cream. He took a ten-minute shower, put on the same pants as yesterday and a casual shirt, and is sitting in front of the TV waiting for his wife, as she needs ninety minutes to get ready. She comes out of the room and asks if the dress looks tight on her. The husband turns and, in a second, says, "Yes." It's the worst news the woman has received in a long time, translated by her as "you're fat." Everything has changed. The ice cream outing, luckily not canceled, now feels like a funeral. She is sad, and she may be for several days. In some circles, they might even start talking about "depression" (I'm exaggerating). All because of a simple "Yes" to a simple question. On another occasion, the wife asks the same question again. The husband, already trained by the previous episode, responds without looking, "Honey, the dress looks great on you." The wife feels loved, and her mood is much happier.

A woman's sensitivity to feeling loved permeates all aspects of the relationship. Even in minor disagreements, the husband must take into account that women interpret things with a different code of interpretation than men. Dr. Emerson references surveys of men and women on how they interpret typical reactions in an argument. The most common reaction in men is to avoid arguing and shut down to avoid problems. A friend once told me that the worst punishment her husband gives her is refusing to talk when she's trying to resolve an issue with him. A survey from the University of Washington confirmed this way of thinking. Women interpret a man's refusal to discuss as highly offensive. Since the matter being discussed is of great importance to her, her interpretation of her husband's unwillingness to talk is that he doesn't love her. It's the worst feeling for a woman.

Women want to feel close to their husbands; they need a connection with them. Even when a woman confronts her partner, she does it to establish a connection, not for the conflict itself. It's understood then why intimacy is just one part of the overall relationship for a woman. She feels uncomfortable with independence and distance because, to her, it signifies a lack of love. Any gesture from her husband that she can interpret as closeness is a pleasant balm for her. Holding her hand or giving her a hug is essential. It's also important for women that their husbands are affectionate without this necessarily leading to sexual relations. After sexual intimacy, a woman expects her husband to continue being emotionally available and close. She might feel it's the best time to discuss important matters, not for him to grab his phone, the TV remote or turn his back to sleep.

Women expect understanding and want to feel that their husbands trust them. Men must learn to listen without feeling pressured to come up with a solution. Many times, women just want to be heard, without expecting the man to immediately brainstorm solutions to their problems. Another thing that matters a lot to women is being in harmony with their husbands. When one aspect of their relationship isn't right, the entire relationship is affected. Women expect their husbands to be gentlemen and affectionate. It's a significant unifying gesture when a man acknowledges his mistakes and apologizes. Apologizing ultimately disarms women. According to wives in my counseling, when a husband apologizes, he gains respect and, with luck, some bonus points.

Women want to reaffirm exclusivity. Husbands must always assure them that they are the only and most influential women in the world. This is expressed through commitment and fidelity. It's important to say it and show it. Husbands should find ways for their wives to see symbols of their love all the time. For example, women generally like flowers. Keeping a vase with fresh flowers in a favorite spot in the house is a way to remind her of her husband's love. When a couple is going through difficult times, the husband ensuring there are always fresh flowers in her favorite corner vase makes the woman feel loved and more willing to resolve the crisis. But we've already talked enough about what's important to women. What can we say about men?

Expecting respect is natural for men, just as expecting to feel loved is natural for women. Wives must consciously demonstrate the respect that their husbands need so much. When a woman is very upset or disappointed, she may say things like, "I have no respect for him." Just as women thirst for love, men seek honor, admiration, and respect. When a woman starts a conversation with words like, "I respect you and have a lot of admiration for you," a man reacts positively to what follows in the conversation. Men want to be respected for their abilities. Women must never forget that a man's work is part of his essence. However, interest in her husband's work should not become an interrogation. Men feel bad when their wives doubt their judgment in work matters and the decisions they make without reason.

One way to show respect to men is to trust in their good judgment. Men want to know that their decisions have their wife's support. In some marriages, it's said and believed that the woman is the one wearing the pants. In such cases, the woman argues that her husband is too passive, and she has to make decisions. There's likely a history behind this passive attitude. When there are differences of opinion, the woman can insist so much on her opinion that the man ends up closing himself off and avoiding confrontation. Repeating these incidents can establish a pattern where the husband always opts for passivity. In some cases, the man insists on taking the lead in an issue and doesn't accept feedback from his wife. One possible result of this attitude is that the husband's weekly menu will be a buffet of bad moods.

Men are "wired" to seek solutions to problems. That's why when the wife is talking about a situation, he doesn't want to hear all the details. He is only interested in the information that allows him to solve the problem. Once he has found a solution in his mind, his focus is no longer on the woman, who is still talking.

Attending to the needs of men is a way to show them respect. And one of these needs is sexual intimacy. For men, sexual intimacy nurtures the relationship, whereas for women, the relationship nurtures intimacy. There's nothing wrong with this; it's just a matter of recognizing the differences. Women like to talk about things to express connections; men enjoy the simple company of their wives in activities they like. Accompanying him while he's watching his favorite football team's game is a way to please him. If the woman remains silent while watching the game together, there's no problem; it's still enjoyable for her husband.

Gender differences enrich marriage. Spouses complement each other and enjoy their relationship when each has what they need most: the other person. Neither of them gets what they want if they don't attend to their partner's needs. It's a poor decision for a man to refuse to show affection and love to his wife when there are disagreements. Similarly, women make a mistake when they punish their husbands in sexual intimacy for issues in other aspects of their marital life.

Expanding upon this topic of gender dynamics in marriage, it's essential to delve deeper into the intricacies of understanding and fostering a strong, loving partnership. The differences between men and women are not a source of conflict but rather an opportunity for growth and mutual support.

Communication plays a central role in bridging the gender gap within a marriage. Men and women often have distinct communication styles. Men may be more direct and solution-oriented, while women tend to emphasize empathy and emotional connection. Couples must recognize these differences and learn to appreciate them. When a husband actively listens to his wife's concerns without immediately offering solutions, it can create a deeper emotional connection. Conversely, when a wife respects her husband's need for space and independence, it can lead to more harmonious interactions.

In many relationships, conflict is inevitable. However, how couples handle conflicts can significantly impact the health of their marriage. Men often prefer to avoid arguments, which can be misinterpreted as indifference by their wives. Women, on the other hand, may want to address issues head-on to establish a deeper connection. Finding a middle ground where both partners feel heard and respected is crucial. Couples can benefit from learning conflict resolution techniques that emphasize compromise and understanding.

Trust is the foundation of any successful marriage. Women want to feel secure in their husband's commitment and fidelity, while men desire to trust in their judgment and abilities. Building and maintaining trust involves open and honest communication, transparency, and a willingness to work through challenges together. A wife's affirmation of her husband's competence and her trust in his decisions can go a long way in nurturing his self-esteem and confidence.

It's important to acknowledge that gender roles and expectations can vary significantly across cultures and generations. Today's marriages often challenge traditional roles, with both partners contributing to various aspects of the relationship, career, and family life. Embracing this diversity and allowing each spouse the freedom to pursue their interests and passions can lead to a more fulfilling and balanced partnership.

Sexual intimacy is another critical aspect of marriage that deserves attention. Men and women may have different sexual needs and desires, but open and honest communication can bridge this gap. Understanding each other's preferences, exploring new experiences, and prioritizing physical intimacy can help maintain a healthy and satisfying sex life.

Ultimately, a successful marriage is built on mutual respect, love, and a deep commitment to each other's well-being. While gender differences are an essential aspect of the relationship, they should not be a source of division but rather an opportunity for growth and connection. Embracing and celebrating these differences while continually striving to understand and support each other can lead to a harmonious and enduring marriage. Remember that every couple is unique, and what works best for one may not apply to another, so open communication and flexibility are key in navigating the beautiful journey of marriage.

VALUES AND SPIRITUALITY

The list of ingredients I have presented in this recipe book for a successful marriage is not intended to be exhaustive. Many other factors contribute to marital satisfaction. I selected these ingredients based on current research on the topic and my experience as a professional counselor. The order of the ingredients does not indicate their level of importance. However, I intentionally left values and spirituality for this moment, as I believe that at this point, you may better understand the previous ingredients, and it is my hope and prayer that they will be helpful and add flavor to the life of my valued reader.

Values are what give meaning to life and serve as the guiding light in the decisions we make. In the words of Dora Tobar, values nourish our interests and inspire everything we do. Essentially, values are always connected to something sacred within a person. Each individual has a list of values that have been shaped throughout their life, nurtured by teachings and personal experiences. When two people enter into marriage, the bride and groom each bring their own list of values. The initial stage of integration, which ultimately leads to the decision to marry, involves comparing these lists of values. When we ask a young woman what she likes about her fiancé, the response typically includes a list of shared values. A typical response might be, "He's generous, gentlemanly, hardworking, spiritual, and noble." It is through the realm of values that an intimate connection with another person is established. The similarity in values is one of the primary reasons that led to the decision to marry and share life together. It's essential to be aware that a person's values can overshadow their flaws. Later in married life, these flaws can become more apparent and potentially poison the relationship. When both partners share the same values, it's easier to reach agreements in various aspects of married life, such as finances, child-rearing, sexual intimacy, and conflict resolution.

When we talk about spirituality, we sometimes encounter a series of stereotypes that don't help us. One of these stereotypes is thinking that spirituality is synonymous with a particular religion. This book is not solely directed at married couples of a specific religious faith. Marriage is a matter for society as a whole, and we want all marriages to be fulfilling, regardless of the spouses' religious beliefs. Another stereotype is assuming that spirituality equates to a set of moral teachings that everyone must adhere to. Since this book is open to all married, divorced, or soon-to-be-married individuals, I'd like to present general spiritual principles that can apply to any religion.

The first principle of spirituality is faith. Marriage is founded on an act of faith. By this faith, two individuals who have no familial relationship, typically met as adults, and have never lived together decide to commit themselves fully to each other and form a new family. If this isn't an act of faith, what do we call it? One must deeply believe in the marital relationship as a path to the desired happiness to undertake it. At the moment of uniting with the other person, there is much excitement and a willingness to build something together. Much is unknown, and there's a lot to discover. In many ways, the famous saying holds true for marriage: "We make the path by walking." The relationship will solidify and adjust throughout life. I emphasize that, regardless of religion, deciding to marry someone is already an act of faith.

Faith in marriage is linked to other values such as family, friendship, fidelity, love, commitment, and sharing. These values have a solid foundation upon which they are anchored. This foundation is the reference point for understanding the entire dimension of love, commitment, fidelity, the individual, peace, and happiness. It is the path that leads us unfailingly to God. Not everything is a mere coincidence. Human life follows a course. To experience movement and appreciate direction, humans need a reference. God then emerges in life as a logical necessity. God explains everything, gives meaning to everything, makes everything possible, and sustains it all.

Research shows that marriages with an active spiritual life also have a solid commitment to their relationship. When applying various scales that measure marital satisfaction to couples, it has been observed that in a considerable number of cases, spirituality is the only scale where the score exceeds 50% of the satisfaction level, while all other aspects of marital life fall within the range of 0% to 20%. Spirituality is the primary ingredient that unifies the flavor of all the other ingredients, ensuring consistency and unity in the final recipe of marriage.

It is essential to understand the role faith plays in each individual's life within the couple and how this faith influences their decisions. In many social circles of modernity, faith and religious matters are labeled as outdated and insignificant. Many couples limit themselves to a civil ceremony to celebrate their marriage and leave no room for spirituality in their marital life because they do not practice any faith individually. Some questions linger. Why is it worth building a family? What comes after this life? Faith helps shape one's relationship with material possessions and interactions with others in society. For a significant number of couples today, faith determines which school their children will attend.

For Christian couples, the education of their children is accompanied by significant moments in the acquisition of spiritual knowledge. The celebration of Catholic sacraments such as Baptism, Confession, First Communion, and Confirmation is preceded by catechesis, which is an actual school of values. Many parents intentionally organize their children's religious education. In many cases, Sunday Mass or a trip to the temple for prayer is the central element of the family's weekly activities. Religions that promote family activities substantially contribute to increasing marital satisfaction.

Spiritual life works miracles in marriages. For example, when a child is seriously ill, their parents take them to the doctor for treatment, but they also seek God's blessing for their child. Blessing each other in the morning when leaving the house and at night before bed are practices of great benefit in family life. Similarly, if spouses choose to pray for wisdom when seeking a solution to a conflict, their willingness to be open to each other is much greater. Spiritual life sets the rhythm of the marital relationship. I cannot conclude this chapter without mentioning how sad it is when some couples use religious activities to avoid interaction at home. They become heavily involved in the church but neglect their marital obligations. It is, of course, a contradiction when one spouse prays a lot but cannot resolve a conflict with their partner.

Values are the compass that guides us in our daily lives, and they become even more crucial when two people decide to build a life together through marriage. These values not only shape individual beliefs and priorities but also influence the shared goals and aspirations of a couple. It's worth noting that while shared values are essential, differences in values can also lead to growth and understanding within a marriage. The process of discussing and reconciling these differences can strengthen a relationship by promoting open communication and compromise.

The concept of spirituality, as mentioned earlier, goes beyond religious affiliations. It encompasses the deeper connection that individuals have with themselves, each other and the world around them. In a marriage, spirituality can manifest in various ways, whether through religious practices, meditation, mindfulness, or simply a shared sense of purpose and meaning. It provides a foundation upon which a couple can build a life together, rooted in principles like love, respect, compassion, and empathy.

One key aspect of spirituality in marriage is the idea of unity and partnership. When a couple embraces spirituality, they often recognize that they are on a journey together, supporting each other through life's ups and downs. This shared sense of purpose can help couples navigate challenges more effectively and find solace in moments of joy and celebration. It's a reminder that their bond transcends the material and temporal aspects of life.

Moreover, faith in marriage isn't just about having faith in each other but also in the journey itself. Marriage is a commitment to growth, adaptation, and evolution as a couple. It's about believing in the potential for love to deepen and mature over time. This faith can serve as a source of motivation to work through difficulties and invest in the relationship's ongoing development.

Incorporating spirituality into your marriage can also lead to a more profound sense of gratitude. Couples who appreciate the spiritual dimensions of their union often find themselves more appreciative of the small joys in life and more resilient in the face of adversity. They recognize that their love is a gift and that nurturing it is a lifelong endeavor.

While spirituality can play a significant role in a successful marriage, it's essential to acknowledge that every couple's journey is unique. Some may find their spiritual connection through shared religious practices, while others may discover it in nature, art, or acts of kindness. The key is to be open to the possibilities of growth and connection that spirituality can offer and to support each other's individual journeys.

Ultimately, values and spirituality are the threads that weave the fabric of a lasting and fulfilling marriage. They provide the foundation upon which a couple can build a life filled with love, understanding, and purpose. By nurturing these aspects of your relationship, you can create a marriage that not only stands the test of time but also continues to flourish and deepen with each passing day.

COMMITMENT

If values and spirituality are the foundations upon which all other elements for a successful marriage are built, commitment is the cement that keeps spouses within the marital project. The end of commitment logically signifies the end of the relationship, in other words, divorce. The University of California, Los Angeles, conducted a study on the meaning of commitment for married individuals. They discovered that it's easy to stay committed to the marriage when things are going well. When that's the case, it's easy to give a testimony like this: "I'm committed to my marriage because I enjoy it." But the true test of commitment lies in words like these: "My marriage is going through difficulties. Changes and sacrifices need to be made. I am committed to this relationship to the extent that I will do everything in my power to make things work." This feeling means that one is willing to do things they don't necessarily like but will do them for the sake of the relationship. Here, commitment is more profound. Couples willing to make this kind of commitment are more apt to resolve conflicts and don't readily think of divorce.

There's no doubt that during their married life, couples experience differences, difficulties, and conflicts. Depending on their severity, these experiences can threaten the very existence of the marriage. This is where commitment to the relationship becomes crucial. The person who wants to save the relationship in the long term is more open to resolving differences or changing their perspective to mend things and resolve the conflict. Some basic techniques can be used to work on saving the marriage. The first is seeking consensus. Here, the goal is to negotiate and find a middle ground where both can live. The second technique is keeping communication channels open during conflicts. Unfortunately, many couples resort to silence when problems arise.

In some cases, they even temporarily or permanently separate bedrooms. This way of acting does not help with commitment. Communication must continue. Of course, not all aspects of shared life are in conflict at the same time. Conflict should not be generalized when the issue at hand is well-defined. There's something magical and unique about marriage. Amidst conflict and crisis, spouses continue sharing the same room, the same bed, and the same sheet. This is a display of commitment to the relationship.

As I am nearing the end of the ingredients section, I would like to take the conversation to another level. Up to this point, I have talked about conflict as the greatest threat to married life. We have said that commitment is the cement that holds everything together; therefore, as long as this commitment prevails, even if disagreements are inevitable, conflict remains optional. Being in conflict is a decision the couple makes. To avoid conflict, one must also avoid managing marital interaction as if it were a bank account where the record of all "transactions" between spouses is maintained. The banking mentality clearly marks gains and losses. Avoiding losses and maximizing gains is how the world of investments operates. Living by rehashing past mistakes and blows is not a way to live in marriage. Regarding this topic, I refer you to my book, "Forgive to Live," published in April 2016.

In over 90% of marriages, people marry with the sincere desire to remain committed to their relationship for the rest of their lives. I have encountered a few cases where someone confesses to not having any commitment on their wedding day. Some of these marriages are rushed due to pregnancy or because the wedding celebration was already prepared to avoid scandal. It must be acknowledged that maintaining commitment is not easy. A classic case is infidelity. Studies have found that the pain caused by infidelity can reach the same level as the death of a loved one. In fact, it is the death of trust in the partner. Discovering sexual abuse of a child, perpetrated by one of their parents or a relative, reaches the same level of pain as betrayal. I could cite more examples. These scenarios destroy the values that give meaning to marriage, and commitment to the relationship becomes very difficult and sometimes even impossible. However, there is no doubt that in these difficult times, the relationship can be saved only through commitment to the marriage.

Commitment is undoubtedly a vital ingredient for
marital satisfaction.

Commitment is often described as the bedrock of
a successful and enduring marriage. It's the
unwavering dedication and loyalty that partners bring
to their relationship, even when faced with the trials
and tribulations that life inevitably throws their way.
When couples commit not only to the good times but
also to weathering the storms together, they
strengthen the bonds of their union.

In a world where relationships can be seen as
disposable and short-lived, genuine commitment
stands out as a beacon of hope and resilience. It's the
willingness to stand by your partner's side during the
darkest hours, to work through problems instead of
running away from them, and to invest time and effort
in nurturing the love that brought you together in the
first place.

One aspect of commitment that deserves special
attention is the idea of compromise. In any marriage,
there will be differences of opinion, conflicting
desires, and moments of tension. Commitment means
being willing to find common ground, negotiate, and
reach compromises that both partners can live with.
It's an essential skill in maintaining a healthy and
thriving relationship. Instead of insisting on being
right all the time, couples who commit to compromise
can find solutions that honor both individuals' needs
and values.

Another crucial facet of commitment is communication. Effective communication is the lifeblood of a marriage. When couples keep their lines of communication open, they can address issues as they arise, prevent misunderstandings from festering, and ensure that they remain emotionally connected. Commitment means not retreating into silence or avoidance when problems surface but actively engaging in dialogue to find resolutions and maintain a solid emotional connection.

Moreover, the idea of commitment extends beyond the individual relationship to the broader context of family and community. Couples who are deeply committed to their marriage often become role models for their children and inspire those around them with the power of love, dedication, and resilience. They show that a lasting, meaningful partnership is possible, even in the face of adversity.

It's important to acknowledge that commitment is not a one-time decision made at the altar. It's an ongoing process that requires nurturing, effort, and a willingness to adapt to changing circumstances. Just as the world evolves, so do the dynamics of a marriage. Commitment means being flexible and responsive to the changing needs and aspirations of both partners as they journey through life together.

In conclusion, commitment is the enduring force that keeps a marriage vibrant and thriving. It's a choice to love, honor, and support your partner through all of life's challenges and joys. When couples embrace commitment, they create a strong foundation upon which their love can grow, flourish, and withstand the tests of time. It's a testament to the enduring power of love and the potential for lifelong happiness in the institution of marriage.

SELF-AWARENESS

In 1978, a scholar named Bowen published a theory. According to this theory, individuation is the process by which a child emotionally and intellectually separates from their family of origin in order to attain emotional maturity and prepare for relating to others. From this theory, some conclusions can be drawn. For example, a person with high self-esteem can handle autonomy and intimacy. In practical terms, this means that such a person can have good relationships without losing their sense of security. Bowen's theory categorizes such individuals as having a high level of individuation. These people are generally pleasant in their interactions, not jealous, and not afraid to confront conflicts to resolve them.

On the other hand, the other side of individuation consists of insecure individuals who cannot separate autonomy from intimacy. Insecurity creates a lot of anxiety and stress in their relationships. They are the jealous people who smother their partners and end up suffocating the relationship. These individuals blame others for their misery and have unrealistic expectations. Beware when someone says, "I can't live without my partner." Some typical attitudes of these individuals include emotional aggression or isolation. They cannot handle the demands of intimacy and also do not accept their autonomy. According to Bowen's theory, these individuals have a low level of individuation.

The process of individuation should culminate in emotional stability, which is the ability to distinguish between emotional processes and intellectual processes. Four factors determine a person's level of individuation: the ability to have one's own personal stance within a relationship, the ability to detach emotionally, fusion with others, and the ability to react emotionally to external factors. It is during youth that a person acquires a certain level of individuation. If someone waits until their wedding day to try to be themselves, it may already be too late. Obviously, we have to consider that others also help us be ourselves in the sense that they challenge us and reflect our own being. Jean-Paul Sartre used to say that the other is the mediator between me and myself.

Given that the self is positioned in front of others, some scientists have discovered a triangular dynamic within relationships that plays a role in determining emotional stability. The basic triangle consists of the mother, the father, and the child. But beneath the surface, there are alliances within this triangle. Many times, the mother is the ally of the child, and the father is left alone. In other instances, the mother is allied with the father, and the child is left alone. Therefore, in reality, the foundation of this triangle is the mother, as she is the one who forms and breaks alliances within the family. Signs of marital dissatisfaction, in this case, include an uncontrolled fusion of intellectual and emotional processes. When people within a couple are confused in the sense that nobody knows who they are, the level of marital dissatisfaction is high.

Self-knowledge is the key to being able to control emotions and reactions within the marital relationship. No marriage dissolves due to intellectual differences. All human relationships are governed by emotions. It is in the emotional realm that satisfaction in a romantic relationship is measured. Everything is negotiated through emotions. The person who wants to understand and care for their marital relationship pays attention to the different active emotions. To connect with the other person's emotions, one must first understand the functioning of their own emotions. The management of emotional processes is the foundation of each person's behavior. Emotional self-awareness is definitely the secret ingredient of every marriage.

Expanding on this topic of self-awareness and its significance in relationships, it becomes evident that a deep understanding of oneself is essential not only for marital harmony but also for all interpersonal connections. The ability to navigate the complex web of emotions, both within ourselves and in others, lays the foundation for healthy interactions, whether in friendships, familial relationships, or professional settings.

Self-awareness goes beyond simply recognizing our feelings; it encompasses an awareness of our thoughts, beliefs, and values that influence those emotions. It involves introspection, reflection, and an ongoing journey of self-discovery. When we have a clear understanding of our own emotional triggers, insecurities, and biases, we are better equipped to communicate openly, empathize with others, and resolve conflicts constructively.

In the context of marriage and romantic partnerships, self-awareness can be a safeguard against toxic patterns of behavior. When both partners in a relationship possess a high level of emotional self-awareness, they are more likely to engage in empathetic listening, express their needs and desires honestly, and provide emotional support to each other. This leads to a deeper emotional connection and resilience in the face of challenges.

Moreover, self-awareness can help individuals identify and break free from destructive relationship dynamics that may have been learned from their family of origin, as mentioned earlier. Recognizing these patterns and consciously choosing healthier alternatives can lead to personal growth and the transformation of relationships.

But self-awareness isn't only about looking inward. It also involves cultivating the ability to perceive and understand the emotions and needs of others. This empathetic capacity is crucial for building strong bonds and resolving conflicts peacefully. By acknowledging the emotions and perspectives of others, we create an environment of trust and mutual respect.

In essence, self-awareness is a journey that encompasses a lifelong commitment to personal growth and the enhancement of our interpersonal skills. It's about gaining insight into the complexities of human emotions, which are at the core of our interactions. By nurturing self-awareness, individuals and couples can embark on a path toward deeper connections, improved communication, and more fulfilling relationships.

So, whether you are in a romantic partnership, nurturing friendships, or navigating the intricacies of family relationships, remember that the quest for self-awareness is not only a gift to yourself but also a gift to those around you. It is a journey worth embarking on, as it has the power to transform not only your relationships but also your overall well-being and personal fulfillment.

RECIPES

DEALING WITH IN-LAWS AND EXTENDED FAMILIES:

- Embrace cohabitation with your in-laws.
- Safeguard the independence of your newfound family unit.
- Foster a relationship of respect with your in-laws and siblings-in-law while maintaining healthy boundaries.
- Prevent direct interference from your in-laws in your relationship.
- Allow your in-laws and siblings-in-law the time they need to adjust to your presence in their lives.
- Invest your effort in getting to know your in-laws.
- Demonstrate your affection for your partner to your in-laws and siblings-in-law.
- Engage in activities with your extended family that they enjoy.
- Stay attentive to their needs.
- Refrain from feeling jealous regarding your partner's relationship with their parents and siblings.

EFFECTIVE COMMUNICATION:

- Continuously regulate the tone of your voice.
- Seek opportune moments for meaningful conversations.
- Articulate your desires and thoughts with clarity.

- Avoid accusations and unfounded assumptions.
- Listen with empathy.
- Honor your partner's viewpoint.
- Nurture trust within your partnership.
- Steer clear of insults or belittling comments.
- Avoid making sweeping generalizations.
- Do not evade discussions on crucial matters.
- Maintain an open disposition toward reaching a compromise.
- Clarify when you feel misunderstood.

CONFLICT RESOLUTION STRATEGIES:

Carve out dedicated time and space for constructive dialogue.

- Keep the channels of communication wide open.
- Extend respectful listening to your partner during disagreements.
- Acknowledge your own contribution to any issues.
- Explore various solutions with an open mind.
- Seek common ground.
- Eliminate options with significant disparities.
- Display willingness to amend your stance.
- Be open to finding a middle ground.
- Refrain from harboring resentment towards your partner.
- Respectfully express your dissent.
- Celebrate conflict resolution as a milestone.

FINANCIAL PLANNING:

- Develop a transparent budget encompassing income and expenditures.
- Decide on the structure of your financial accounts.
- Allocate responsibilities for managing these accounts.
- In cases where both partners work, determine each individual's contribution to household expenses.
- Establish a dedicated savings account.
- Allot a portion of the budget for personal expenses.
- Exercise restraint when it comes to credit utilization.
- Consolidate your debts and establish precise repayment methods.
- Strategically plan for major expenses such as vehicle purchases, furniture, or vacations.
- Keep financial accounts accessible to both partners.

ENHANCING SEXUAL INTIMACY:

- Define the frequency of sexual encounters through open discussion.
- Engage in conversations regarding each partner's desires and preferences.
- Refrain from using excuses like exhaustion or excessive workload.

- Avoid using sex as a bargaining chip within the relationship.
- Ensure that expressions of love and affection are not solely tied to sexual activity.
- Strive to maintain a genuine and emotionally connected sexual relationship.
- Understand that not every display of affection needs to culminate in sexual intimacy.
- Cultivate robust communication regarding your sexual relationship.
- Respect your partner's boundaries and consent.
- Continuously provide constructive feedback on this aspect of your relationship.

SHARING RESPONSIBILITIES:

Allocate tasks based on each person's skills and interests.

- Extend mutual support to one another.
- Equitably distribute household chores.
- Avoid gender-based assignments of responsibilities.
- Collaborate actively in executing various household tasks.
- Involve children in age-appropriate household responsibilities.
- Actively participate in shared household tasks.
- Remain adaptable and open to necessary changes.
- Approach household duties with enthusiasm and positivity.

MUTUAL SUPPORT AND ENCOURAGEMENT:

- Exhibit genuine interest in your partner's life.
- Strive to gain a deep understanding of your partner.
- Encourage and support your partner's aspirations and dreams.
- Respect your partner's opinions, even in cases of disagreement.
- Participate in activities your partner enjoys.
- Assist your partner in setting goals and priorities in their life.
- Foster creativity and innovation within your partner.
- Avoid making hasty judgments.
- Acknowledge and celebrate your partner's strengths and accomplishments.
- Offer unwavering support to help your partner overcome their fears.
- Become your partner's greatest advocate and cheerleader.

THE COMMITMENT YOU OWE EACH OTHER:

- Embrace your partner with their unique qualities and limitations.
- Refrain from making comparisons with others.
- Preserve the sanctity of your relationship by refraining from speaking negatively about your partner to others.

- Approach every challenge with a team mentality.
- Seek consensus and compromise as guiding principles.
- Abandon the need to always be right.
- Show kindness and grace even during times of disagreement.
- Be willing to make sacrifices for the greater good of your relationship.
- Never intentionally cause harm or suffering to your partner.
- Steer clear of habits that could jeopardize the bond you share.
- Listen actively and attentively to your partner.
- Demonstrate your understanding of your partner's emotions and feelings.

WORK:

- Leverage your work to enhance your marriage.
- Collaboratively decide who will work outside the home and who will manage household responsibilities.
- Understand the impact of work on your relationship.
- Prevent your marriage from becoming a weekend-only affair due to work commitments.
- Respect each other's equal rights to pursue professional careers.
- Ensure that all family members contribute to the well-being of the household.

- Avoid using work as an excuse to avoid quality time with your spouse.
- Recognize that work is not the root cause of infidelity.
- Prioritize your marriage over the demands of your job.
- Remember that earning a salary does not grant sole authority over financial matters.
- Be mindful of warning signs in your marriage, such as fatigue, lack of energy, anxiety, and irritability.
- Establish mechanisms for rest and vacations.

EDUCATION:

- Embrace the importance of education for every individual.
- Acknowledge that education can reduce poverty rates and mortality.
- Recognize that education fosters better communication skills.
- Understand that education is a cornerstone of equality.
- Embrace education as a means to achieve your dreams.
- Appreciate how education contributes to an improved quality of life.
- Leverage education to access better employment opportunities.
- Recognize that education plays a role in ensuring financial stability at home.

- Understand that education offers children a brighter future.
- Encourage your children, regardless of their gender, to pursue education.
- View education as an avenue to a better world.

GENDER: FOR MEN:

- Create a safe space for your wife to express her feelings without feeling attacked.
- Consistently demonstrate love and affection towards your wife to meet her emotional needs.
- Respect your wife's emotional sensitivity.
- Actively participate in household chores.
- Cultivate affectionate gestures that do not rely solely on sexual intimacy.

FOR WOMEN:

- Avoid dwelling on past mistakes when communicating with your partner.
- Demonstrate the respect and admiration your husband deserves and desires.
- Refrain from using manipulation or emotional outbursts to express your needs.
- Be attuned to your husband's need for intimacy.
- Communicate your emotions in a way that fosters understanding rather than confrontation.

- Avoid criticizing your husband or inundating him with your emotions.

FOR BOTH:

- Embrace and respect each other's differences without diminishing one another.
- Establish open and respectful channels of communication to discuss your feelings.
- Prioritize addressing, responding to, and resolving issues promptly.
- Continuously show appreciation for each other.
- Understand that some level of disagreement is natural and acceptable.
- Promote equality within your partnership.

FRIENDSHIPS:

- Refrain from making your partner choose between you and their friends.
- Maintain your friendships even after marriage.
- Show respect for your partner's friendships.
- Recognize your partner's right to maintain their own friendships.
- Familiarize yourself with your partner's friends without feeling obligated to befriend them all.
- Strike a balance between your friendships and your partnership.

- Encourage each other to have individual friends while also cultivating shared friendships.
- Ensure that friends do not intrude upon your marriage.

Leisure Time:

- Cultivate opportunities for enjoyable activities.
- Pursue personal hobbies and interests.
- Create shared leisure activities as a couple.
- Offer mutual support for each other's individual pursuits.
- Relive and cherish positive shared experiences.
- Establish a budget for leisure activities.
- Learn to balance social interactions and personal time.
- Engage in wholesome recreational activities that benefit your marriage and family life.
- Organize family-centric leisure activities.
- Set aside time for leisure with friends.

Children:

- Embrace children as a gift within your marriage.
- Understand that children often mirror their parents.
- Recognize that children symbolize a love open to life.

- Appreciate how children infuse vitality and joy into your marital bond.
- Acknowledge that raising children is a collaborative effort in divine creation.
- Understand that the well-being of your children justifies the challenges and sacrifices in marriage.
- View marriage as the ideal platform for nurturing and guiding your children.
- Embrace your roles as your children's first educators.
- Acknowledge the role of marriage in providing emotional stability for children.
- Value family life as the arena for socialization and moral development in children.
- Recognize that your interaction as spouses serves as a model for your children's values and future relationships.

EXPECTATIONS:

- Maintain realistic expectations concerning your partner and your relationship.

EXPECTATIONS REGARDING YOUR PARTNER:

- Prioritize mutual respect.
- Uphold fidelity and trust.
- Offer unwavering support to each other.
- Advocate for equality.
- Express affection consistently.

EXPECTATIONS REGARDING MARRIAGE:

Seek emotional and social stability within your partnership.

Pursue happiness together.

Embrace the rights and responsibilities that come with marriage.

HABITS:

- Embrace both your strengths and weaknesses.
- Accept your partner with their strengths and weaknesses.
- Familiarize yourself with your partner's habits.
- Communicate your preferences regarding their habits, both positive and negative.
- Avoid attempting to change your partner.
- Refrain from criticizing your partner for their habits.
- Extend assistance when your partner seeks help in changing negative habits.
- Avoid making comparisons between your partner and others.
- Embrace and encourage positive habits exhibited by your partner.
- Acknowledge and affirm your partner's efforts to become a better person.
- Refrain from making harsh judgments about your partner's worth based on isolated displeasures.
- Strive to understand your partner's perspective.
- Maintain open lines of communication at all times.

AGREEMENTS:

- Strategically plan when to start a family.
- Collaboratively decide the division of labor regarding work outside the home.
- Organize your finances efficiently.
- Establish clear guidelines for household responsibilities.
- Foster effective channels of communication.
- Discuss and align your expectations for marriage.
- Thoughtfully manage personal, familial, and friendship relationships.
- Prioritize open dialogue regarding sexual intimacy.
- Decide on the arrangement of your living space.
- Cultivate the spiritual aspect of your family life.
- Set boundaries for relationships with extended family members.
- Create meaningful family traditions.
- Coordinate celebrations with other families for significant occasions.
- Reach a consensus regarding interactions with ex-partners.
- Establish conflict resolution strategies.

PARENTING:

- Always collaborate as a united team.
- Maintain a clear guiding path for the upbringing and education of your children.

- Lead by example in your teaching.
- Keep the lines of communication open with your children at all times.
- Cultivate trust and avoid instilling fear.
- Establish firm yet fair rules without resorting to threats.
- Foster meaningful dialogues as a way of connecting.
- Grant your children sufficient freedom for their own learning.

- Avoid making comparisons between your children.

- Acknowledge your own mistakes and learn from them.
- Emphasize the positive aspects of their behavior.
- Strike a balance between being a parent and a friend.
- Provide ample space for your children's growth and independence.
- Be attuned to your children's emotions and feelings.

Self-awareness: To have a fulfilling marriage experience, it's crucial to understand:

- Your unique character and personality traits.
- How you manage and express your emotions.
- Your expectations regarding the institution of marriage.
- Your deeply held values.
- Your preferred communication style and methods.
- Your self-esteem and self-worth.

- The intricate story of your emotional journey.
- The history and dynamics of your own family.
- The influences of your parents' marital dynamics on your own perceptions.
- Your contributions to marriage, including talents, solutions, challenges, and habits.
- The depth of your commitment to the relationship.
- The status of your other significant relationships.
- Your willingness to learn and grow alongside your partner.
- Your personal habits and routines.
- The role of spirituality or religious beliefs in your life.
- Values and Spirituality:
- Recognize that spirituality forms the heart of a successful marriage.
- Practice your spiritual values through daily interactions as a couple.
- Understand that spirituality is the bedrock of conflict resolution.
- Embrace spirituality as a protective shield for your marriage.
- Build your marriage on the solid foundation of shared spiritual beliefs.
- Cultivate meaningful spiritual experiences within your relationship.
- Clarify and respect each other's religious beliefs and practices.
- Establish strategies for imparting spiritual values to your children's lives.

CONCLUSION: MARRIAGE AS THE SCHOOL OF LIFE

Within the realm of education, pedagogy serves as the guiding science. It is not merely a methodology but also an ethos, an intention woven into the fabric of how we impart knowledge. Beyond the mere transmission of facts, it's about nurturing the ability to perceive knowledge from diverse angles and through one's own eyes. The true pedagogue ignites a curiosity for discovery, an affection for newfound knowledge, and the mastery of self-guided exploration. Extending this concept to marriage, we find that no one person holds the role of a teacher. Marriage itself assumes the role of the educator. The journey of a couple unfolds as a unique daily experience, and from it, continuous learning emerges. Those who approach marriage as instructors soon tire and falter, while those who embrace it as an ongoing lesson become its masters. Indeed, marriage possesses its own pedagogical essence.

In the context of traditional education, the camaraderie among students is beautiful. A missed class can be compensated for by sharing notes with a fellow student, fostering an atmosphere of equality. Similarly, a thriving marital relationship is built upon this spirit of togetherness. In a marriage, there is one teacher, which is the marriage itself, and a single cohort of students - the spouses. They share laughter over shared jokes and commiserate over life's injustices. Can you accept that within your marriage, you are nothing less than a lifelong student?

Countless experiences with your partner lie ahead: the ebb and flow of daily interactions, the mundane challenges of life, the joys and tribulations of raising children, the arrival of grandchildren, the onset of illnesses, retirement, and perhaps even the loss of a partner. Each of these life events constitutes a lesson within the school of marriage. I invite you to utilize the wisdom and strategies presented in this book to make the most of every situation. Worry not about graduating with honors; there are no deadlines in this school. Continue to relish your journey of learning and embrace your marriage to the fullest.

In this unique institution of matrimony, the curriculum remains dynamic and ever-evolving. Much like the traditional educational system's progression through grades, marriage entails distinct stages and phases. Each phase introduces a fresh set of lessons, challenges, and opportunities for personal growth.

The initial years of marriage are often marked by the thrill of discovery and the joy of building a shared life. During this phase, you learn the intricacies of cohabitation, the art of compromise, and the establishment of your unique rhythms as a couple. Communication, patience, and understanding become your primary subjects.

As time marches on, you may find yourselves confronted with the challenges of raising children. This phase adds a new dimension to the curriculum, teaching the value of teamwork, self-sacrifice, and the profound love that accompanies parenthood. You discover the delicate balance between your roles as partners and parents, deftly managing responsibilities while nurturing your bond.

The latter stages of marriage usher in their own unique lessons. As both partners age, you confront the changes that come with it. Health concerns, financial considerations, and the empty nest syndrome may become prominent topics in your marriage curriculum. Here, resilience, adaptability, and the ability to find joy in each other's company despite evolving circumstances take center stage.

Throughout this journey, you will encounter tests and assignments that challenge your commitment and devotion. Moments of doubt and uncertainty will arise, but they are also opportunities to deepen your mutual understanding and fortify your connection. Remember that making mistakes is an integral part of the learning process. Similar to a traditional school, wisdom arises from experiences, whether they be positive or negative.

In the school of marriage, there are no diplomas or degrees to be earned. Perfection is not the goal; instead, it is growth. Each day presents a fresh chance to learn, to love, and to cherish the partnership you have built together. Your life partner serves as your fellow student, and together, you navigate the beautiful, unpredictable journey of marriage.

So, embrace your role as a perpetual student of marriage and savor the lessons it offers. Continue to delve into the depths of love, understanding, and companionship, recognizing that there is no final exam, only a lifelong commitment to learning and living your marriage to the fullest.

ABOUT THE AUTHOR

Father Edouard Atangana is a distinguished priest in the Diocese of Brownsville, Texas, celebrated for his steadfast dedication to faith, education, and the upliftment of others. His pastoral and scholarly endeavors reflect his profound commitment to community service.

His academic journey is characterized by both diversity and depth. Father Atangana commenced his higher education with a bachelor's degree in philosophy from the Saint Canisius Faculty of Philosophy in Kinshasa, Congo, in 1994. He then embarked on theological studies, initially at the Pontifical University in Mexico City, before continuing at the University of Saint Mary of the Lake in Chicago, Illinois. There, he achieved a Bachelor's degree in theology, a Master of Divinity, and a Licentiate in Fundamental Theology in 2002.

With a dedication to communication and compassionate care, Father Atangana ventured into the field of Communication Disorders, obtaining a license as a Speech Pathology Assistant in Texas in 2005. His academic pursuits further led him to specialize in Bioethics in 2008, earning a certificate from the National Catholic Bioethics Center in Philadelphia, Pennsylvania, focusing on the ethics of frozen embryos.

In 2015, he expanded his expertise in human behavior, achieving a doctorate in Advanced Studies of Human Behaviors from Capella University in Minneapolis, Minnesota.

As an accomplished author, Father Atangana has published 12 books addressing a range of topics, including adolescent upbringing, forgiveness, marriage, self-development, spiritual growth, gratitude, and ministry to the sick. His books are rich with wisdom, empathy, and spiritual insight, offering guidance through various life stages and challenges.

His qualifications as a Life Coach, a specialist in Bereavement recovery, an accredited professional in Domestic Violence intervention, and a certified Chaplain in the National Association of Catholic Chaplains demonstrate his comprehensive approach to supporting individuals in their spiritual and personal journeys. He is also known for conducting conferences, directing retreats, and leading continuing education sessions in the USA, Mexico, and Cameroon.

Father Edouard Atangana's extensive expertise and empathetic approach to ministry and counseling have solidified his reputation as a unique and esteemed figure in his community and beyond.